AF321528

DIANA MACKIE is a professional painter, born in London and based on the Isle of Skye since 1990. In 1993 she left the island for three years to study for a degree in Interior Design at Edinburgh Napier University. While in Edinburgh, she took the opportunity to develop her ideas in stained glass at the Edinburgh Stained Glass House, and drawing and sculpture at Edinburgh College of Art. On returning to Skye, she received her first interior design commission, including artefacts and garden design, for the Three Chimneys Restaurant with Rooms. Diana's ancestor Samuel de Wilde (1751–1811), whose studio was in Drury Lane, was famous for his theatrical paintings – which now dominate the collection in The Garrick Club, London. Her great grandfather, Captain William Mackie (1839–1887), was captain of the clipper ship *The Ben Nevis*, which on one occasion took the record from *The Cutty Sark* for the fastest Glasgow to Melbourne run. This inheritance is evident in her work: as a painter, she is constantly observing and interpreting the drama of the ever changing weather, often through powerful seascapes. Her art and a film inspired by her work can be viewed at www.diana-mackie.co.uk. Diana's studio and gallery are part of her house at Borreraig, where she lives with her musician husband, Alan, and their dog, Barkly.

Skye
Through an Artist's Eye

DIANA MACKIE

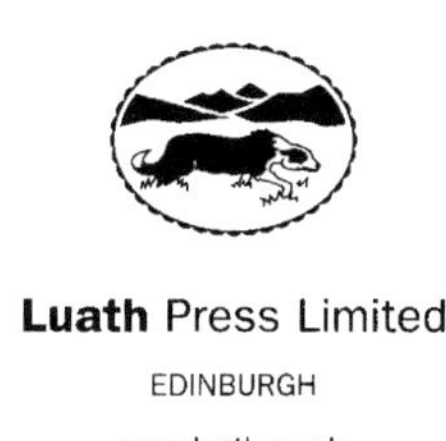

Luath Press Limited

EDINBURGH

www.luath.co.uk

First published 2020

ISBN: 978-1-913025-68-7 jacketed hardback
ISBN: 978-1-912147-67-0 printed paper case hardback
ISBN: 978-1-912147-66-3 paperback

The paper used in this book is recyclable. It is made
from low chlorine pulps produced in a low energy,
low emission manner from renewable forests.

Printed and bound by CPI Antony Rowe, Chippenham.

Typeset in 10.5 point Sabon by Main Point Books, Edinburgh.

All photographs by Diana Mackie unless otherwise stated.

This book is dedicated to Mother Nature,
who never ceases to humble and inspire.

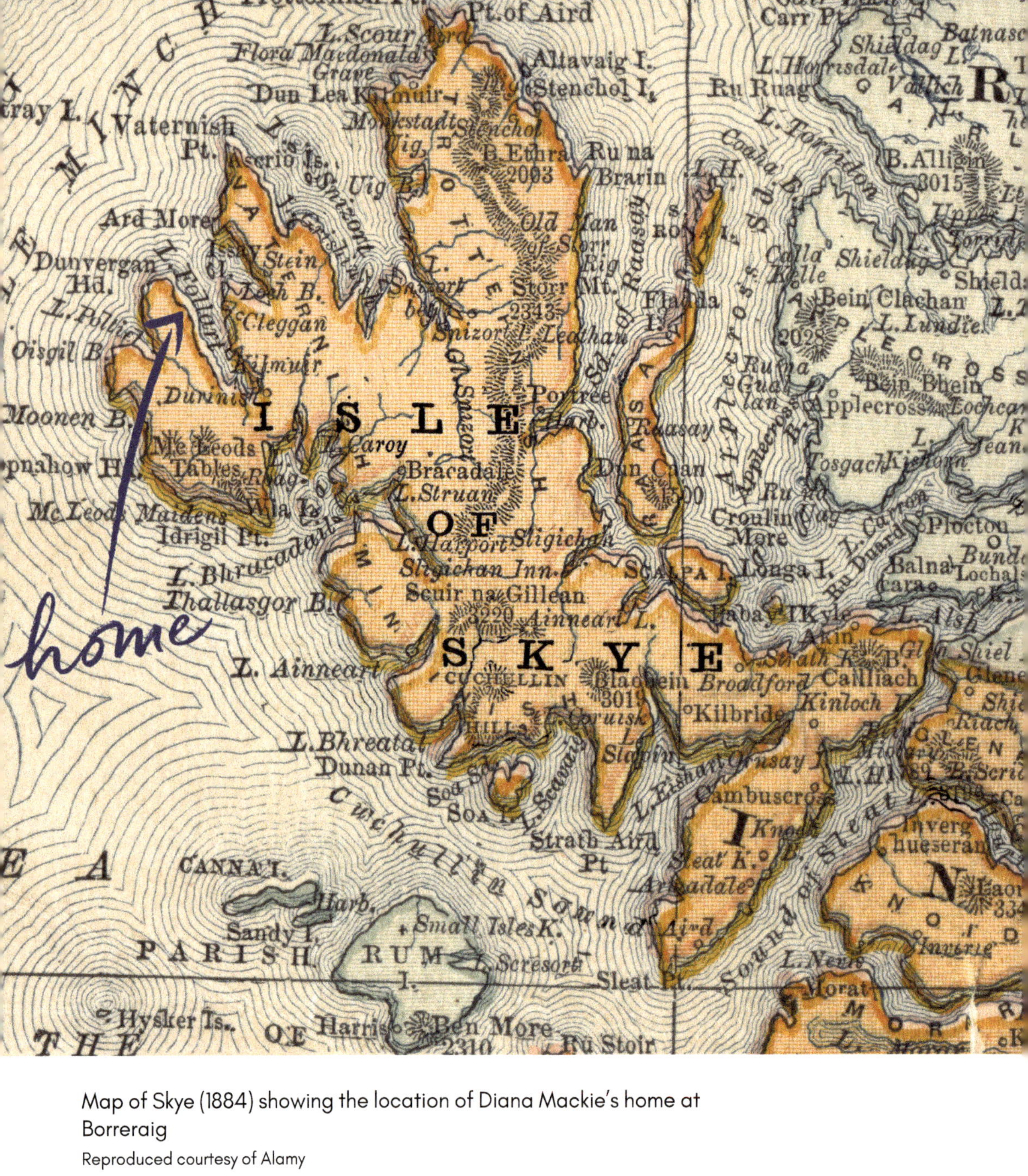

Map of Skye (1884) showing the location of Diana Mackie's home at Borreraig

Reproduced courtesy of Alamy

Contents

Acknowledgements

MY THANKS TO Gavin MacDougall of Luath Press for giving me the opportunity to express myself and my work in this book, and particularly to Jennie Renton who has skilfully guided me through this first publishing experience.

I am eternally grateful to Edinburgh Napier University for including me as a mature student in their Interior Design degree course, a training which was life-changing. I am also most grateful to Shirley Spear OBE and her husband Eddie Spear, who gave me my first major design and art project, and to Scott Ross, marketing manager of The Three Chimneys, who has given me so much encouragement. Thanks are also due to Graphic artist Peter McDermott, who helped me source the old map of Skye reproduced in this book and who wrote 'home' on it with such a flourish.

I must thank a number of photographers for their input: Ewen Weatherspoon for his many years of photographing my paintings and for his permission to reproduce these images in this book; Adrian Hallister for his photograph of the wreath laid on the shore of Loch Ewe in memory of all who lost their lives during the Arctic Convoys; Merlin Aerial Photography for permission to reproduce two aerial views of our home; and Eamonn McCabe for his photograph of me at my easel.

Peter Harrison and his family, owners of the Pool House Hotel, Poolewe, have given invaluable information about the Arctic Convoys. Thank you for sharing your boundless knowledge relating to this period of our history.

Andrey Pritsepov, former Russian Consul General, had so much empathy and enthusiasm for the concept underlying the triptych of paintings which I have donated to the Arctic Convoys Museum in St Petersburg.

My daughter Amy Simmons, poet and film critic, whose words and observations I hold in the highest esteem, helped me realise the idea of making a book. On my walks round Skye, our rescue mongrel Barkly has been my delightful companion. Finally, huge thanks to my crazy, adorable husband, Alan, whose ridiculous sense of humour has carried me through the most frustrating of times.

Home lights candles in the dusk,

Where we drink the night and

Cast nets on broken shores.

Amy Simmons

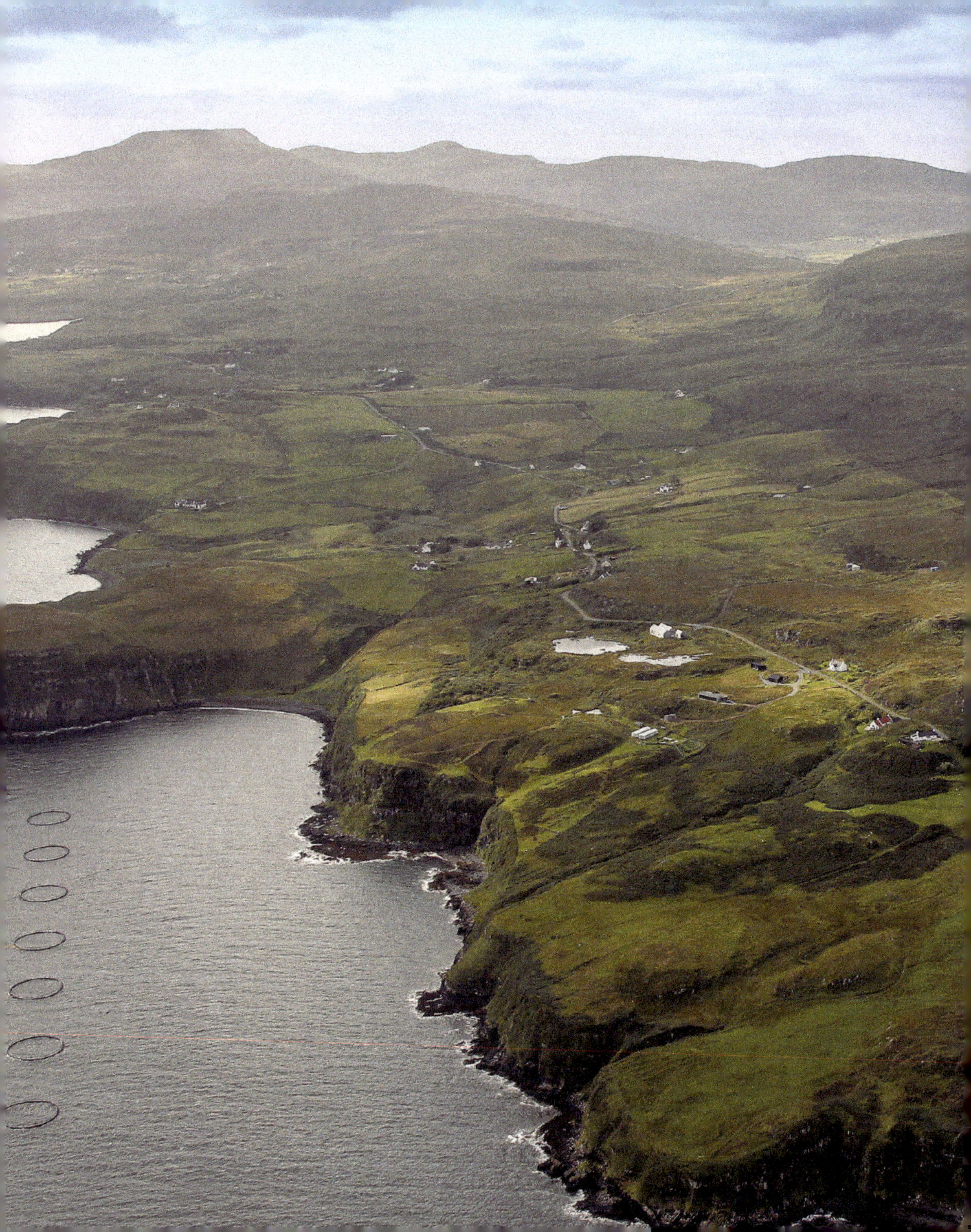

Introduction
The Isle of Skye: A Living Palette

SKYE, THE LARGEST and northernmost of the major islands in the Inner Hebrides, has been occupied from the Mesolithic period, leaving a historic trail of artefacts for the archaeologists to discover. Well into the 20th century it was occupied largely by crofters, whose way of life was extremely harsh by today's standards – even into relatively modern times. It is startling to realise that electricity only became available to most of the island's inhabitants as late as the 1950s. I was once told a lovely story of an elderly lady who, in the early days of electricity, was visited by the meter man. He could not understand why her usage was so low. Her response was that it was wonderful to have the electricity, as she could now see to light the oil lamps when it was dark!

The island is full of reminders of its past inhabitants, not least those who were forced to depart during the notorious Clearances of the early 19th century which took place all over the Scottish highlands. Local lairds 'cleared' their tenants to make way for sheep, which had become far more profitable than the rents collected from the crofters, who barely subsisted from their smallholdings. As a result of this 'unrelenting avarice', as Sir Walter Scott described it, over a period of about 40 years Skye's population fell from 20,000 to just under 9,000. There are many heart-breaking tales of the brutality that was commonplace in forcing people from their homes. They then endured harrowing journeys to America or Canada, packed together in conditions of terrible privation in small emigrant sailing ships, some surviving the crossing, others not. Stone ruins of

Left: Aerial view of Diana Mackie's house and studio at Borreraig
(third inlet down)
Image: J Martin Phillis

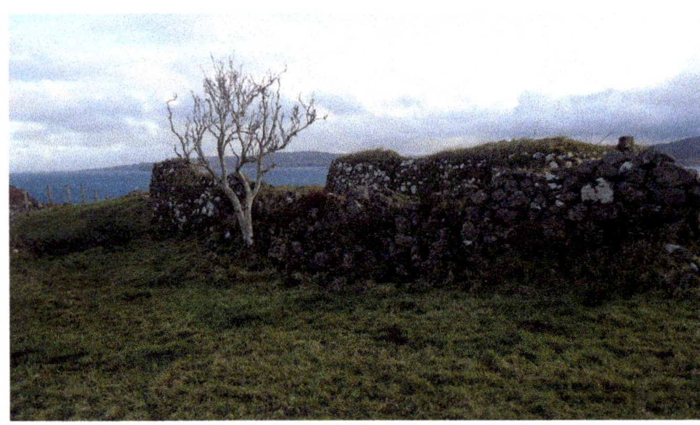

Rowan and ruin, Galtrigill

their deserted homes scattered over the landscape of Skye echo their passing.

I am intrigued the atmosphere of the deserted village of Galtrigill and the ruined houses of Borreraig. I often wander among the tumbled stones, imagining these deserted townships as they once were. I think of the people who lived here, eking out a living from the land, living on the edge in every sense. How closely attuned they must have been to the yearly weather cycle.

As an artist, I too continually observe weather patterns, the way the light changes, how conditions affect the land; but for them, this acute awareness, this 'reading' of land, sea and sky, was a matter of necessity rather than aesthetics, informing an understanding that would determine their patterns of work, how they tended their crops and animals and when to fish.

There is an unlimited supply of fresh water at Galtrigill, thanks to a robust burn that never dries, even in the hottest of summers. And there are large rocks that would have made good drying areas for clothes and blankets on sunny days.

An old path leads from the ruined village to a tree-lined gulley. From there, I go down to the shore via stone steps worn into curves by the feet of generations of people making their way to the fishing boats on the shore, or perhaps to the smokehouse. A large cave at the far end of the bay intrigues me. What part did it play in their lives? It is now all so quiet, bereft of human habitation, just the sounds of nature, from the sea to the rustling of leaves and the babbling burn.

I often stand at the water's edge watching the sea, then make my way along the tideline, beachcombing for configurations of shade, form and texture that might provide inspiration for my paintings.

Back in the deserted village, I often sit under a rowan tree, remembering that rowans were always planted near a house as it was thought that the colour of the red berries would ward off evil spirits. I have a few in my garden… you can never be too sure of anything.

As I sit, I imagine the sound of the voices of the crofters going about their business in their moment in time. The sound of youngsters, playing, chanting. A dear elderly neighbour of mine remembers stories of badly behaved children being told to stand on the 'naughty stone' in front of the whole village. I wonder which stone might have been the naughty stone in days gone by. All around, homes that must have held love and heartache are gradually being absorbed back into the ground. It is the emotion of passing lives that I am so affected by, nature supporting us for a period of time only. I can't help but wonder, for how long?

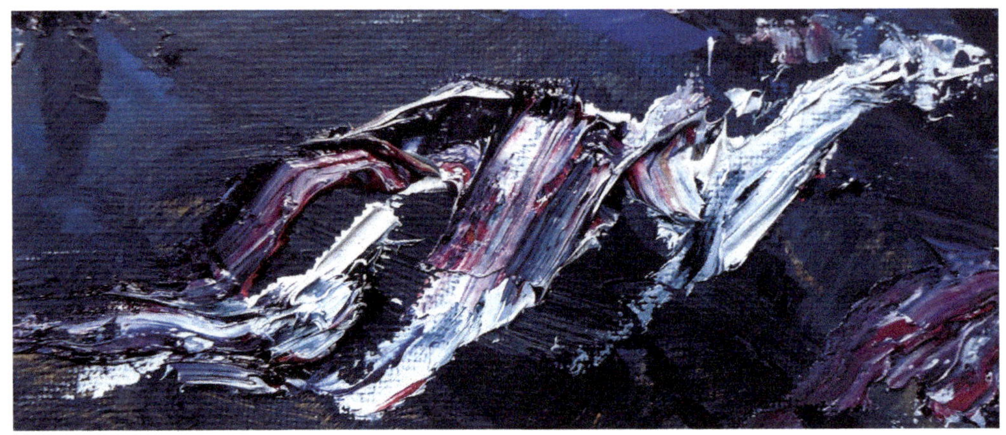

An Artist's Formation

ONE OF MY earliest recollections is of sitting on my mother's knee in front of the kitchen fire at our house in Pinner. I remember being given a sweet, which for our household was a very special occasion. All my senses were on alert as I held the prize between my fingers. The wrapper was colourful, crackly and squeaky. Oh, the pleasure of it all! I unwrapped the sweet very carefully. Holding it in one hand and the wrapper in the other, I gazed on my treat with glorious anticipation. Unexpectedly, I then placed the beautiful coloured paper in my mouth, leaned forward and threw the sweet on the fire.

In more ways than one, this was a sign as to the way my life was to go.

My father was extremely proud of his vegetable plot in our back garden, so to be allowed a pocket handkerchief of hallowed soil to plant seeds in generated a feeling of enormous gratitude and reverence in me. As a child, my fascination with nature was never less than intense. I used to marvel at seed heads, their patterns and how they would move in the breeze. I still feel amazement that a grainy seed can produce such outcomes.

My place of escape and fantasy was a gap in the hawthorn hedge at the bottom of the garden, where a hard soil floor carefully swept with twigs gave me my first sense of making a place for myself. Orange boxes were used for tables and cupboards, while my parents' empty gin bottles acted as vases. Creating this living space – which I now see as my first venture into spatial design – gave me a sense of security, a feeling that has never dulled in its importance for me.

I have memories of endless summer days rushing around the garden, dressed in my pale blue, hand-knitted swimsuit with a felt bunny on the front, armed with a brass bug spray. This weapon gave me unimaginable powers. Anything that was squirted by me would be changed into anything I wished, or transported to another place. Everything in the garden was a victim of my imagination.

Rainy days were spent indoors, drawing and painting. I spent a great deal of time and care over studies of birds' feathers, showing how they overlap and how the wings change when they open. Paper and paint remain an area of escape in which there is always a degree of magic going on.

My Scottish grandfather was based in Glasgow but rented a cottage for the family in Benderloch, Argyll, where we spent many glorious summer holidays.

The cottage was situated opposite the most picturesque railway station you could ever imagine.

Going up to Scotland on the night sleeper was hugely exciting. We would board the *Royal Scot* or *The Flying Scotsman* at King's Cross. The vast roof of blackened glass arrested the belching smoke and returned it back along the steaming giants and their carriages. The station echoed with the distorted sounds of announcements over the tannoy, slamming doors, shouting guards and shrill whistles, heralding the beginning of a journey.

I remember my father once walking me along the platform to introduce me to the giant of an engine, which was fed by piles of coal situated behind an engine driver black with coal dust. He acknowledged our presence with a grin that displayed incredibly white teeth. I will never forget the acrid smell and the heat the engine gave off, the hissing monster jetting out steam with such force you would lose sight of the great wheels, which rose higher than the top of my head. My father bent down to say, 'Just think of it, this engine is going to take us all the way to Scotland.' I couldn't imagine it was possible to travel any further to anywhere.

I was taken to a sleeping comp-artment where I was allotted a bunk bed and told very firmly that I should not open the window. Left alone, I gave my full attention to my surroundings, including the large china pot which was to be emptied through a trapdoor under the wash basin.

It was time to open my brown suitcase and take everything out, gaze at the contents and decide what would occupy me first: my beloved Edward Bear (I loathed dolls), crayons, pencils, paper, notebooks, *The Observer's Book of Birds*, or I-Spy books.

With much hissing, steaming and clanging, we pulled out of the security of the station. As darkness fell I was fascinated to see from the window horizontal smoke filled with glowing cinders, leaving a magical trail behind passing trains. I was keen to know if our engine was doing the same. A wide leather strap had to be wrestled with to let the window down. It would only be a question of pulling it up again, no one would know, I told myself. The window crashed open and the leather strap all but vanished in the mechanism and cold, smoke-laden air rushed in. I spent as long as I dared looking out at a wonderland of dark and light, speed and smoke. I then had to pull up the window and go back to bed, which was not so easy. I just could not manage the weight of the

window with the tiny piece of leather strap that was protruding. All I could think of to say was, 'The window… it just fell down.' When my parents looked in on me, I pretended to be fast asleep, but my smoke-smeared face told the true story.

The house at Benderloch had a backdrop of steep hillside covered in trees and bracken. We would collect our drinking water from a spring-fed pool just below a sizeable cave, where, we were told, a hermit used to live.

It took a while to get used to bath-time. I loved the cosiness of the bathroom with its sloping, wood-lined walls. I never quite got used to the brown, brackish water which gushed from the taps like well-brewed tea, accompanied by peaty bits and pieces that would float around me.

Golden eagles nested in the rocky outcrops directly above us. I loved watching them as they wheeled about on unseen thermals. Ever since those highland summer days, I have always adored the smell of sea, peat and wet ground. I remember standing on the edge of the sea loch, holding my father's hand and watching the seals pop their heads up to have a good look at us, while he told me about the Roman burial ground that we were standing on.

The western highlands, a place

of such beauty and wild, dramatic landscapes, so different from my home in the suburbs of London, would remain in my heart forever. Little did I imagine what part Scotland would play in the rest of my life.

Painting and drawing became my only joy through my miserable teenage years. It became obvious to the school and my parents that I was not destined for any profession, so it was deemed that I must become a receptionist or a hairdresser. In making this judgement, there was never any reference to my artistic ability. Training in Art would have been seen as Bohemian and not likely to lead to a 'proper job'.

I was duly enrolled in a two-year hairdressing City and Guilds course at Tottenham Technical College. The Tottenham Hotspur ground at White Hart Lane was just down the road from college and I became a Spurs fan, spending my Saturday afternoons on the terraces listening to the tribal banter. I was beginning to feel that I was at last able to climb up the sides of my protective parental barrel to have at look at real life.

There were art classes as part of my course and – joy! – visits to the London galleries. I fell in love with Turner and Gainsborough. I adored Stubbs for his beautiful images of horses and dogs, Rembrandt for his colour palette and use of light and, of course, the Impressionists and their radical use of paint.

In college we spent a day a week drawing intricate historical hairstyles. The idea was that we would eventually sit beside our clients and sketch potential hairstyles for them. However unlikely this outcome, I hugely enjoyed the detailing of the hair.

My own drawing and painting had taken second place and this continued after college, when I went on to work very long hours in various hairdressing salons. Although not my career choice, this served me well during my married life when times were tough.

My choice of husband was no doubt in reaction to the conventions of my middle-class upbringing. Handsome, worldly and very left wing, he introduced me to jazz, which I had never been exposed to at home. He was 17 years older than me and my parents were not happy, to say the least. But it was my choice.

After my daughter Amy's birth in 1972, I was able to attend classes run by our local council. I studied silversmithing, pottery and sculpture. I was finally able to create by modelling with clay, and studies of perspective and mark-making opened up another magic box. One of my tutors said to me: 'Whatever mark you make, make it interesting.'

How true.

Difficult years lay ahead. My husband was a printer with *The Times* and after Margaret Thatcher and Rupert Murdoch set to work on the print unions, life seemed to revolve around redundancies and strikes. Families suffered and we were one of them. The marriage did not bear the strain. I then spent some impecunious years in London. In 1990, some friends offered me a rent-free bolt-hole in Skinidin. I decided to take the leap into living the life of a full-time artist, albeit in an unimaginably remote township in north-west Skye.

I had never before set foot on the island. I arrived in October at the start of one of the worst winters in living memory. The croft house was in a terrible state of disrepair and overrun with mice. The gales generated the most terrifying sounds as they howled through the loose guttering and ill-fitting doors. I decided to make the most of the precious daylight with my camera and sketch book, and started to explore, soaking up the drama and beauty of this extraordinary island.

I spent hours studying and to my great joy I read for the first time John Ruskin's *The Elements of Drawing*, in which he writes:

> …never force yourself away from what you feel to be lovely, in search of anything better, and gradually the deeper senses of the natural world will unfold themselves to you in still increasing fullness of passionate power…

Before leaving for Skye, a dear friend had given me the gift of a canvas and some oil paints. On one of those dark nights when the gales were hammering and I was playing some favourite opera pieces at full blast, I found myself getting out the oil paints. I have never returned to watercolour – my new-found medium was capable of translating my surroundings with the appropriate drama. I was on course for a voyage of discovery.

Some friends had encouraged me to apply to university, an idea that filled me with dread. Nonetheless, despite no previous success academically, with a sort of blind boldness I convinced myself that I had nothing to lose. I was offered a place in Interior Design at Edinburgh Napier University and graduated three years later, with the class medal, at the age of 50.

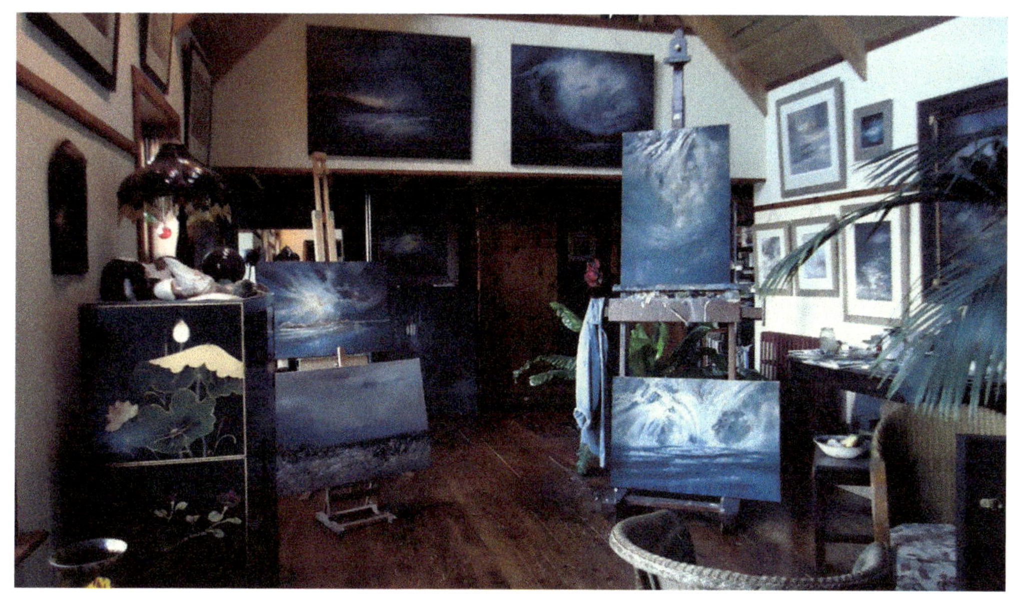

The Studio at Borreraig

I LIVE IN Borreraig, a few miles from Dunvegan on the north-west coast of Skye with my musician husband Alan and our much loved rescue dog, Barkly. Our house is perched above a beach close to the mouth of Dunvegan Loch. From our front windows we look northwards across to the white shore-line of the Coral Beach and to the Outer Hebrides beyond.

Our home started life as a two-up two-down croft. With its deep stone walls and an atmosphere all of its own, its past life resonates with our present. Jessie, the previous owner, lived there alone. A much loved member of the community, she kept a cow and sheep, plus a few chickens. Very kindly towards her many nephews and nieces, she has left us a legacy in the form of visits from her many relations over the years. They drop in for a cup of tea and tell us stories of the fun they once had here: prising limpets from the rocks and frying them on the kitchen range;

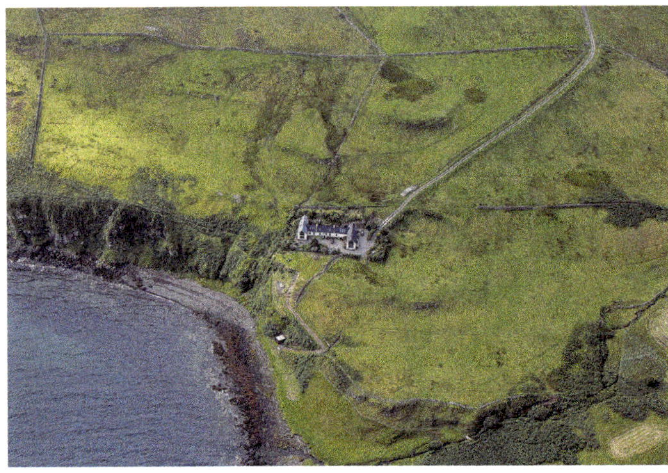

Aerial view of Diana
Mackie's house and studio
at Borreraig
Photo: J Martin Phillis

fishing from Fisherman's Rock; and running races down the steep hill from the broch behind the house, bouncing down through the heather.

The house itself has always felt at peace to me. It has a distinctive smell that I was afraid of losing with all the additions we have made to it. But I am pleased to say that whenever I open the front door there remains the slightly musty, woody smell which was there when the place first welcomed me.

There are now two generous extensions, which I designed myself. I find it is such a special experience to draw a space that you will eventually walk through and work in. The high ceilings to accommodate the largest of easels hitherto could only be dreamt of, but it happened!

I did not want to overwhelm the old place with modern design, I wanted to embrace it in the form of a farm steading: the new wings extend on either side of the original structure, offering a protected internal space.

I believe a design for a building should reflect the history of the environment and be sympathetic to the landscape it will occupy. I have always enjoyed old churches and schoolrooms, and lots of exposed roof space.

My studio is home to work in progress. I never fail to enjoy the reactions of visitors as they pass through our low-level snug and enter

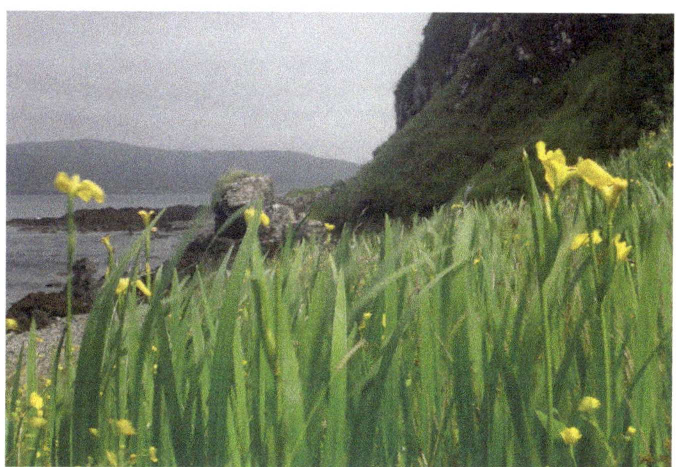

Wild irises on the beach
at Borrreraig

this high-ceilinged space, which is dominated by my extremely large and paint-spattered easel, the air permeated with the smell of turps and oil paint.

An enormous palm stands in one corner, in front of my Mondrian-style stained-glass panel, which runs from first floor height to the floor. I situated it on the south side, where the sun can project through the strong colours onto the old gable end of the cottage. It is magical to see these colours ebb and flow as they change in shape, form and intensity.

A fern stands on the floor, spreading its broad leaves and enjoying the north light from the generous skylights. I have always found indoor plants companionable, especially in the winter when it's dark and cold. These tropical plants seem to be very much at home within the environment I am offering them.

Large windows look out to sea and across to the moors, giving a sense of connection with the paintings. I also have a gallery area where finished works are hung in a more formal style. All these years have gone by and I still have to pinch myself that this is really happening.

Winter is the time when we are on the receiving end of ferocious storms channelling their way through the mouth of the loch, gales hitting our windows full on, which is a bit unnerving but we are quite used to it.

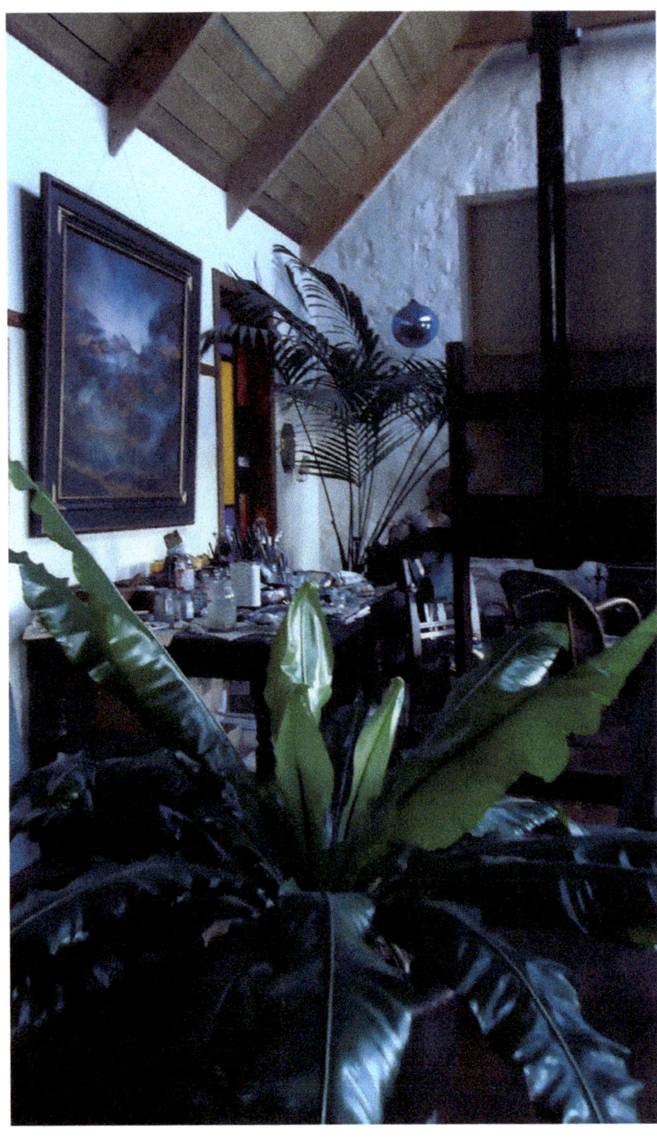

Companionable plants in the studio

It is the daily observation of how light and weather change through the seasons that gives me so much to draw upon. Every day is a masterclass from nature. Cloudscapes present a world of penetrable landscape, subtle in tone, dynamic in shape, sometimes in colours you can hardly believe, as the light from sun and moon play within the clouds. My focus is fixed when I see shafts of sunlight penetrating through dramatic cloud banks, or the full moon in the night sky.

Every morning Barkly and I go down to the beach below our house. On my first step outside, I take a huge breath of salt-laden air, quite as good as a glass of champagne; in fact, better. Barkly's passion is seal-watching – while otters are quite elusive, seals are nearly a daily

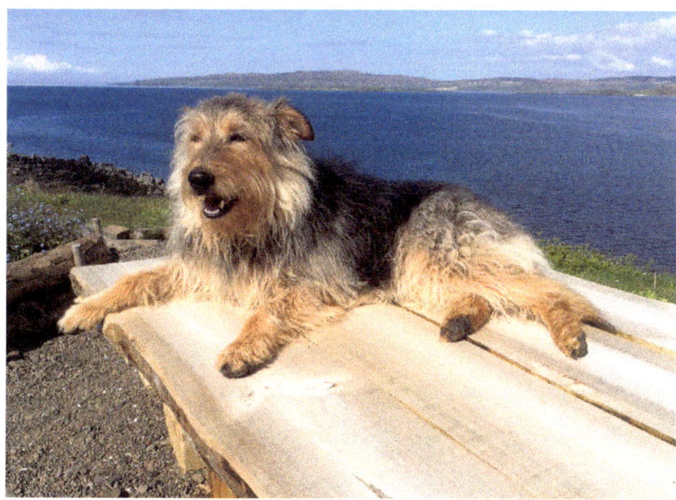

Barkly at the beach

occurrence. When a seal appears they both maintain eye contact for a few seconds, then the seal will vanish underwater only to reappear further down the beach, seemingly playing hide and seek, while Barkly rushes up and down the tideline, barking encouragement.

The beach is a source of great pleasure for observing the movement of the waves. I sit in my 'hide' and look for hours at how they form in varying degrees of power, depending on the weather conditions; how they break against the rocks, showering plumes of spray up onto the cliffs. I watch closely as they gather out to sea to finally curl over and rush up the beach and then retreat with a resounding rattle through the pebbles to make way for the next wave, in a sequence that has been repeated since time began. Rather like the universe, it is too much to comprehend. As I watch the sea from this beach, I am always mindful of the broch and the deserted village above me, and imagine the ghosts of its inhabitants watching me – strangely, in no way an uncomfortable feeling.

Easel

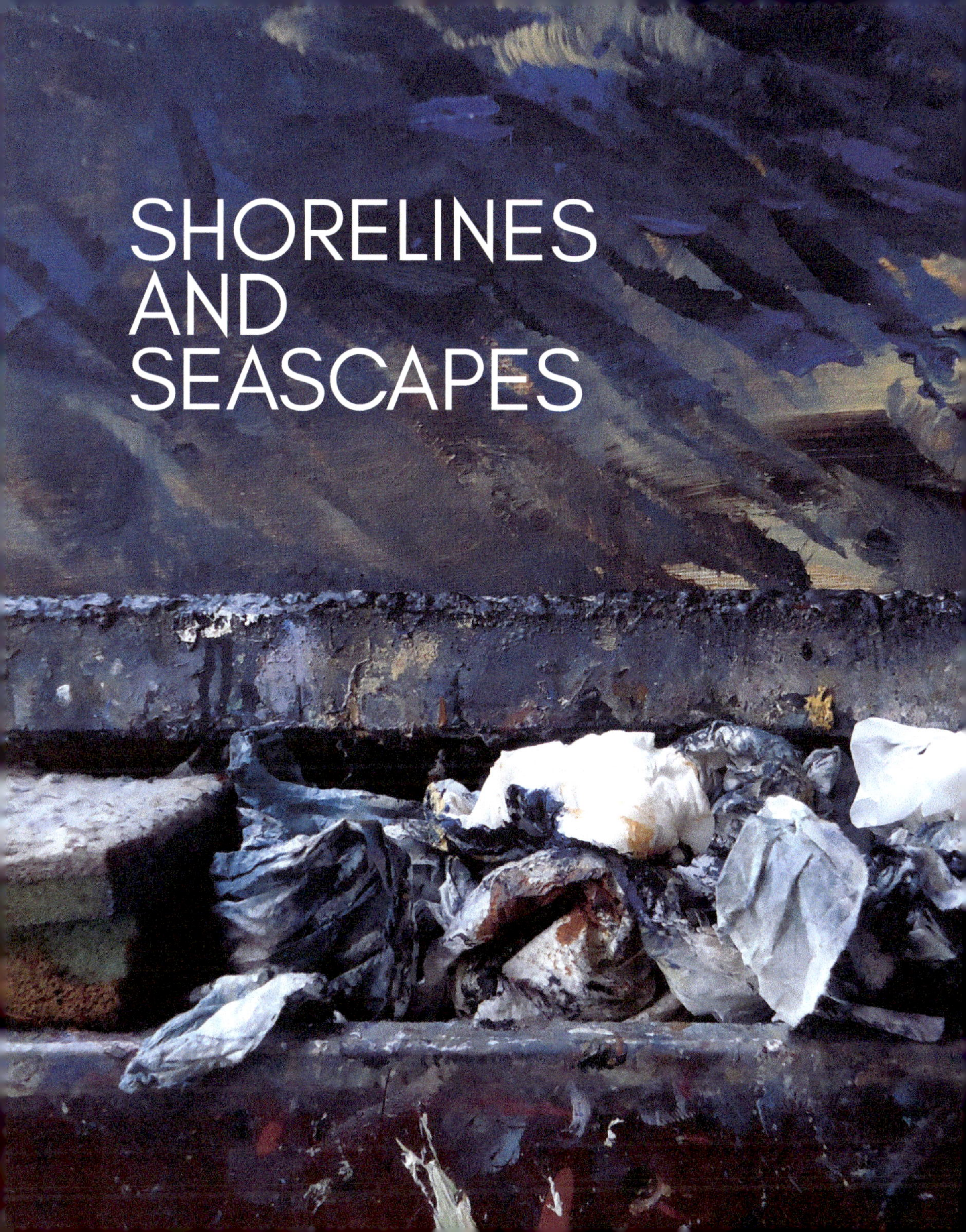
SHORELINES
AND
SEASCAPES

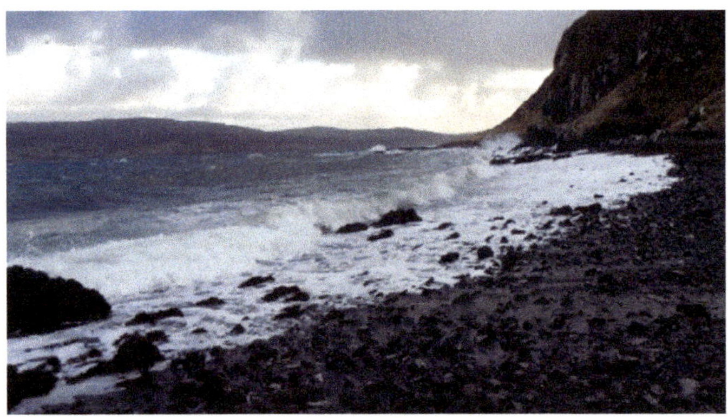

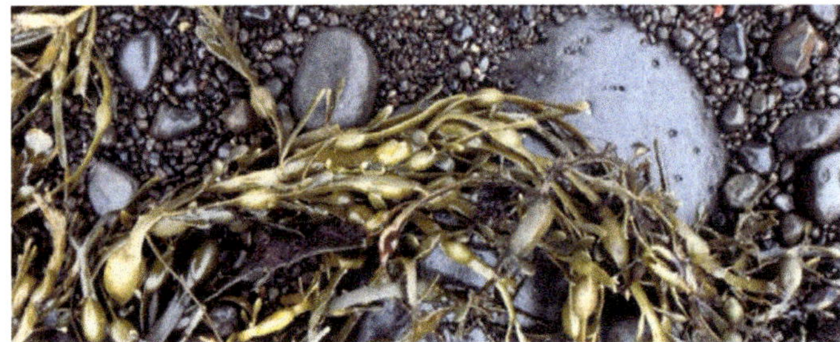

Shoreline, Borreraig

WHEN I FIRST arrived on Skye 29 years ago, I would spend half of every day sketching, taking colour notes and photographs to aid the memory of the day. I am particularly fascinated with cloudscapes. They seem to have a life of their own, either enormous and static like huge mountain ranges, or scudding independently through their own domains.

From a painterly perspective, the challenges are endless when bulk and fragility, transparency and movement need to be conveyed within a cohesive landscape study. I would never paint from a photograph. Oil paint is for me the most expressive of mediums to work with. There is such a range of application, from thick palette mark-making to the thinnest of washes. Probably I would offend the purist but my feeling is, if it works, do it.

I have worked in watercolour for many years and enjoy the mixing of colour and the variety of papers. Some of these wash techniques I have

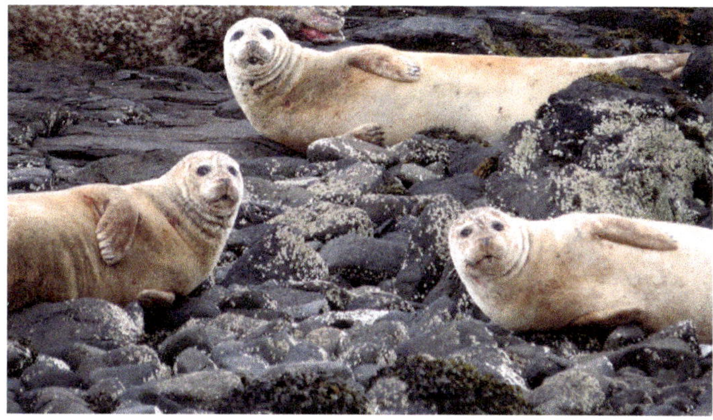

Seals
Photo: Stephanie Taylor

also used in my oil paintings. It is a continual quest to find the right application to create that bit of magic to bring a painting to life. I use a variety of tools apart from brushes, including sponges, old credit cards, broken twigs and screwed-up paper, to mention a few.

I constantly store up visual images relating to Skye. Every day, a new weather condition will present its own colours, tones and subject matter. Autumn and winter give me the greatest inspiration. They offer great beauty and mystery, forms veiled in cloud or mist – it is always what you can't quite see that I find the most interesting. It leaves an area in the painting for the viewer to make their own private imagined journey.

Perhaps the place I have painted more than any other on Skye is Coral Beach; certainly I have painted it in all weathers. It lies 40 minutes down a track from the car park at Claigan. As you emerge from the woods, there are some ruined stone buildings: an old sawmill, stables and a coach house that are now firmly closed off to the public, but many years ago I spent a couple of days inside them, sketching. I made two watercolours of these interiors – my last use of watercolour.

With every step as I walk to Coral Beach I feel an increasing sense of detachment from everyday concerns, as sky, sea, coastline, moor and mountains share their moods with me. Off the coastline between Dunvegan Castle and Coral Beach is a scatter of tiny islands that are usually dotted with seals. It is quite ridiculous how tame they are.

The track to Coral Beach was the scene of a dramatic rescue involving my great friend Jeanette Bryant. Her treasured pet goose, Will, had been blown away in a storm and she was losing hope of ever seeing him again, when someone phoned while I was visiting to report sighting a goose on the beach.

We immediately headed off in the fading light, only to find the gate to the beach path locked. Undaunted, Jeanette's husband lifted it off its hinges and as we drove along, the whiteness of Will's feathers was picked out in the car's headlights.

The scene that followed was worthy of Disney. Jeanette leapt out of the car, tears pouring down her face, her arms outstretched. Will responded by opening his wings and waddling furiously towards her. But back in the car, Will went completely limp and we all feared the worst. He turned out to be made of stronger stuff than we thought, and he made a full recovery.

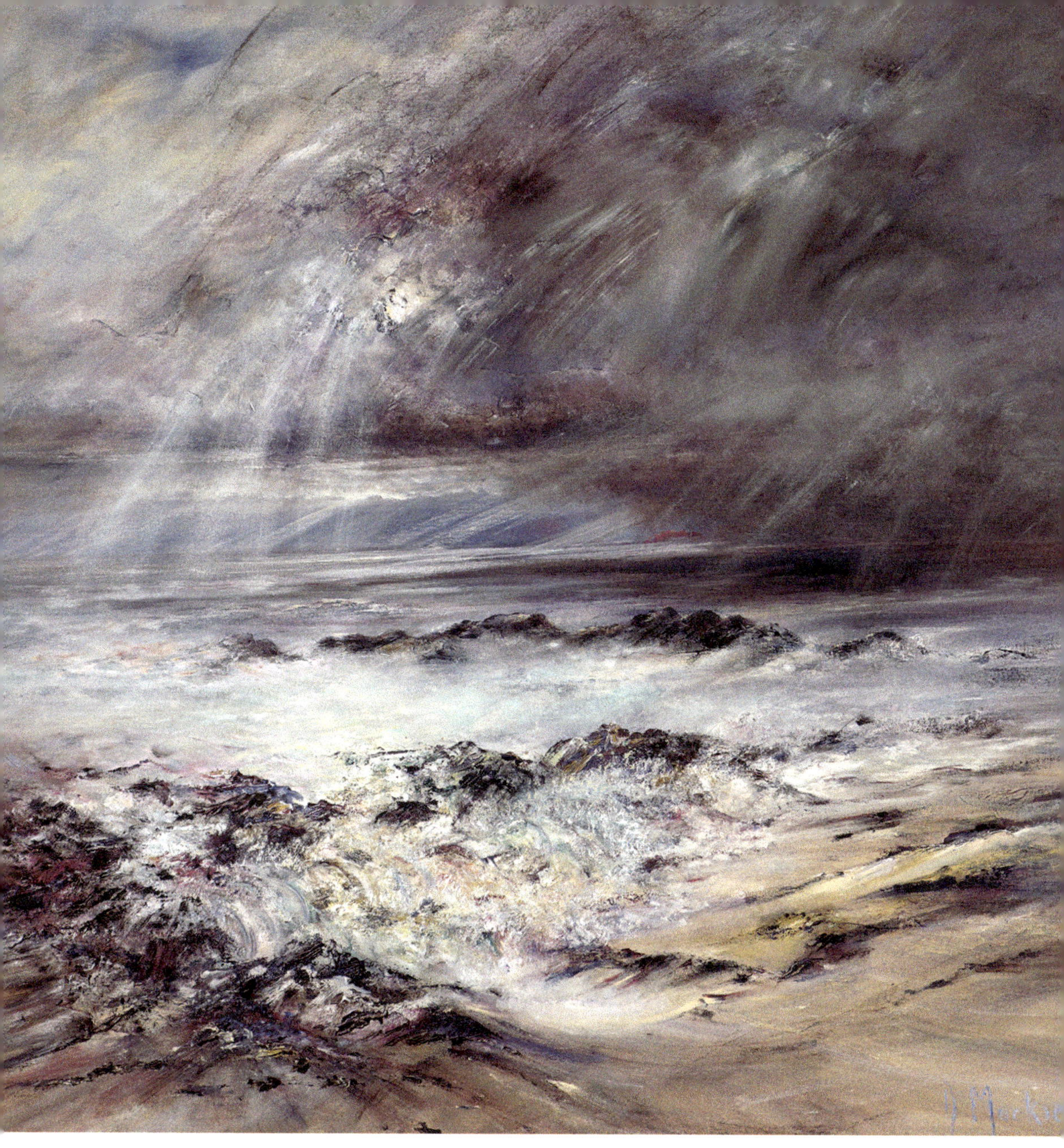

Change in the Weather, Coral Beach, Claigan

With such a huge skyscape you can witness every oncoming weather front.

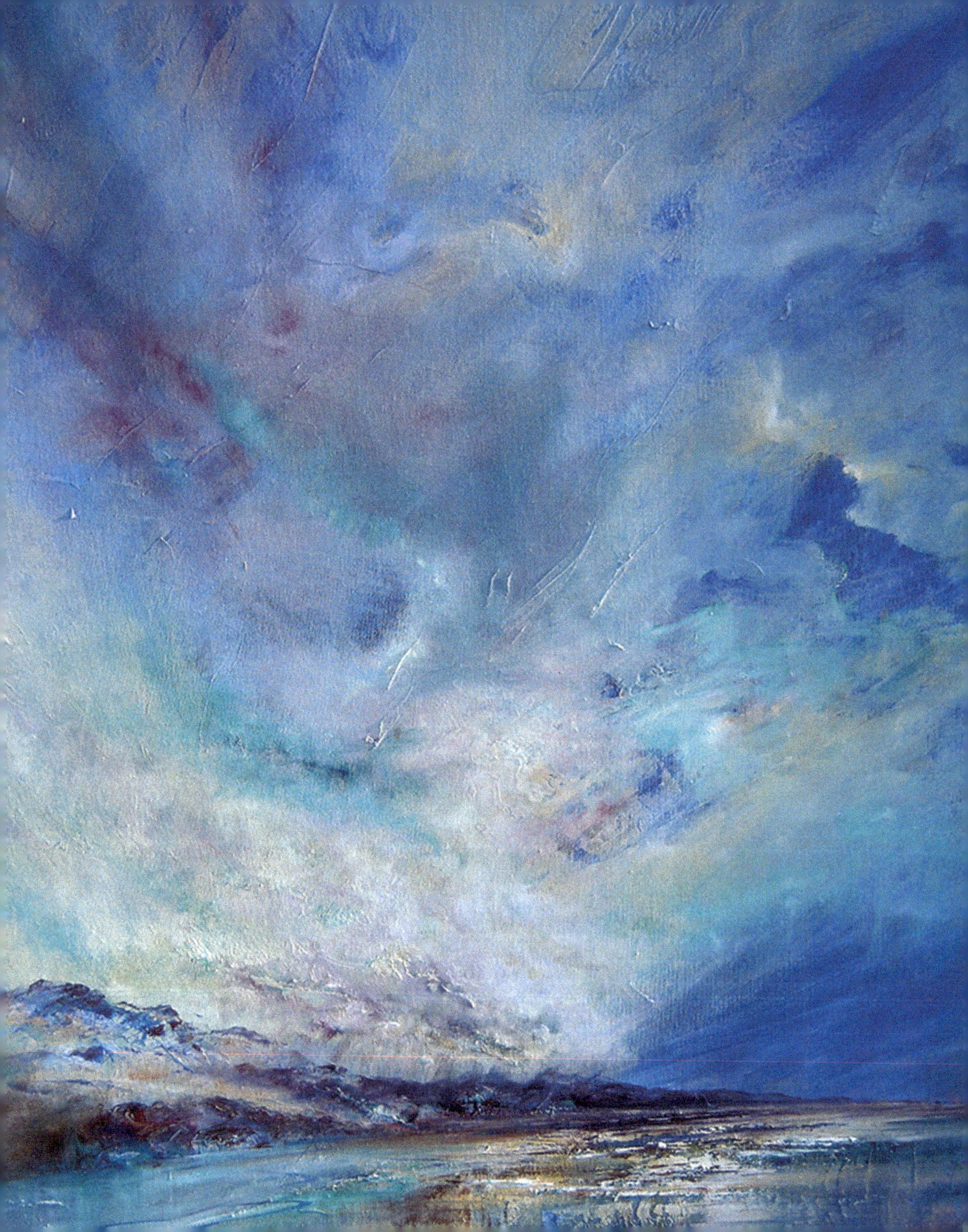

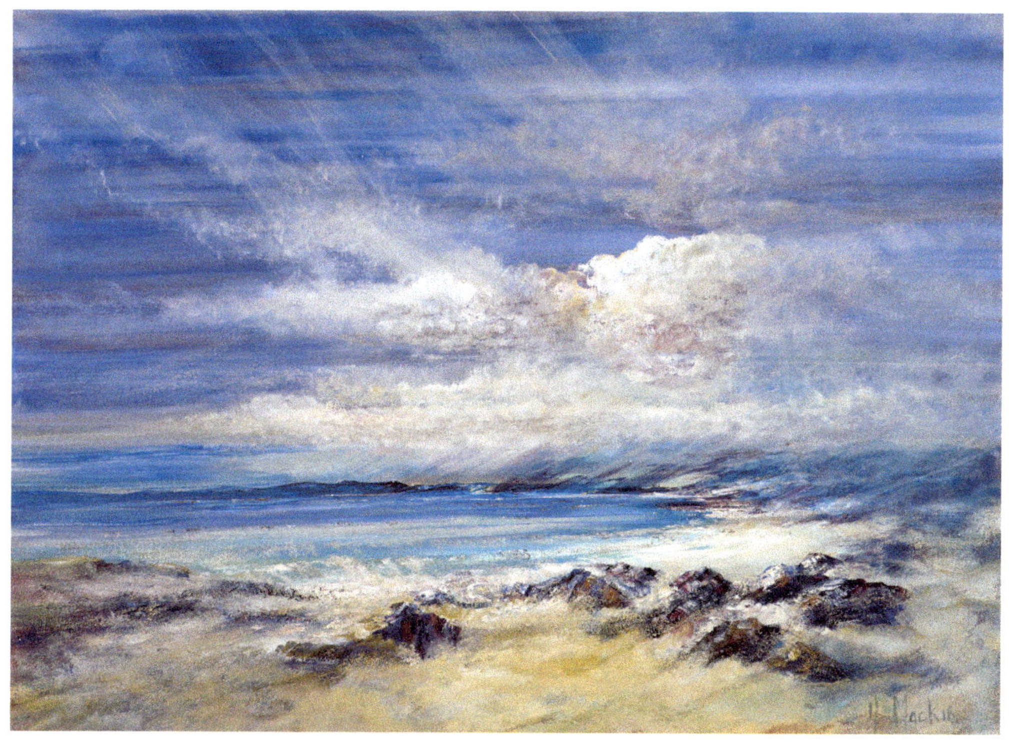

Coral Beach, Early Morning (left)

Huge blue skies, the promise of a good day. A calm sea with plenty of texture to aid the reflections.

Coral Beach in Summer (above)

Blue sky, blue sea, warm beach.

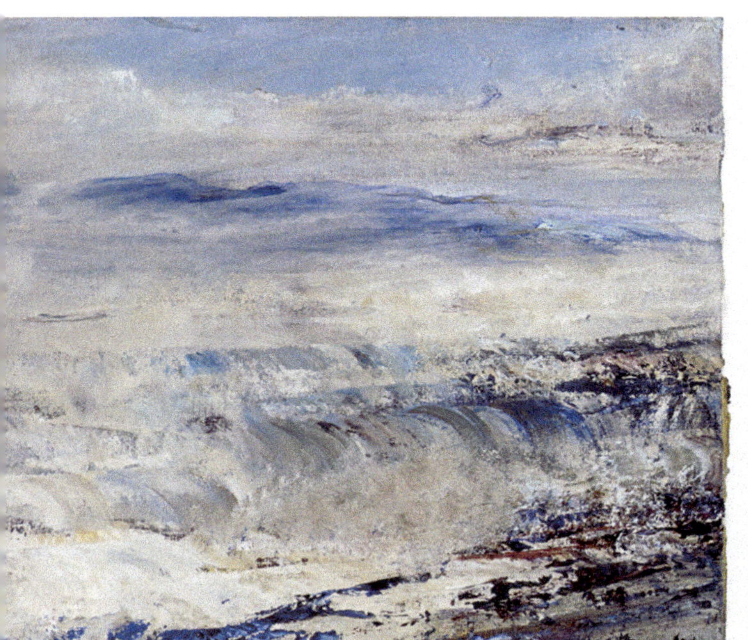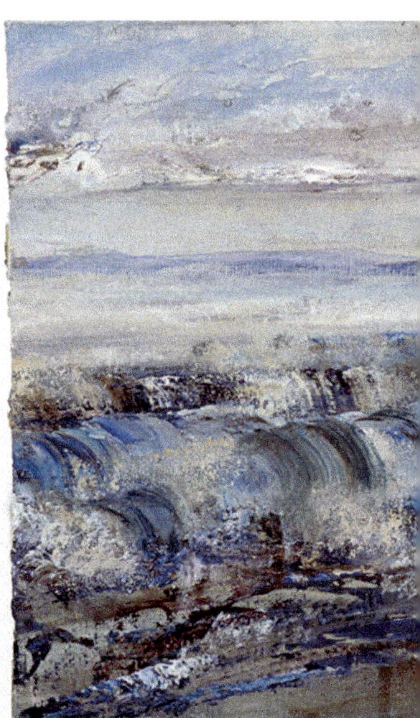

Spring Tide at Coral Beach, triptych

I have painted many impressions of this place, reflecting my many seasonal visits. On this occasion, I chose three separate canvasses to convey the length of the beach. It is interesting how the eye fills in the gaps between each painting. Interpreting the misty spray from the waves proved to be a challenge. The optimistic blue sky with scudding clouds is so typical of a bright but changeable day on Coral Beach.

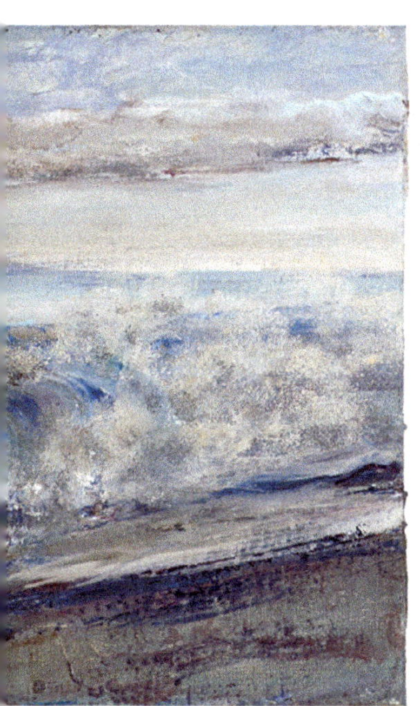

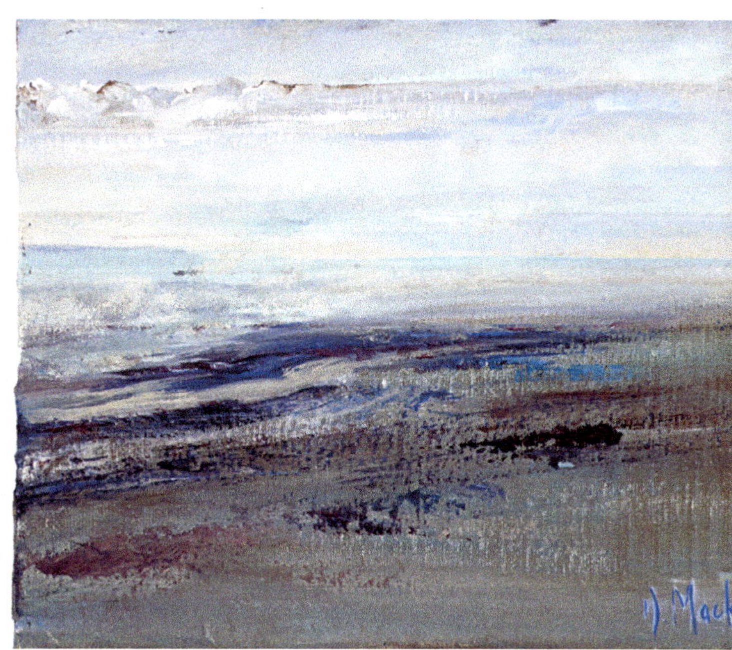

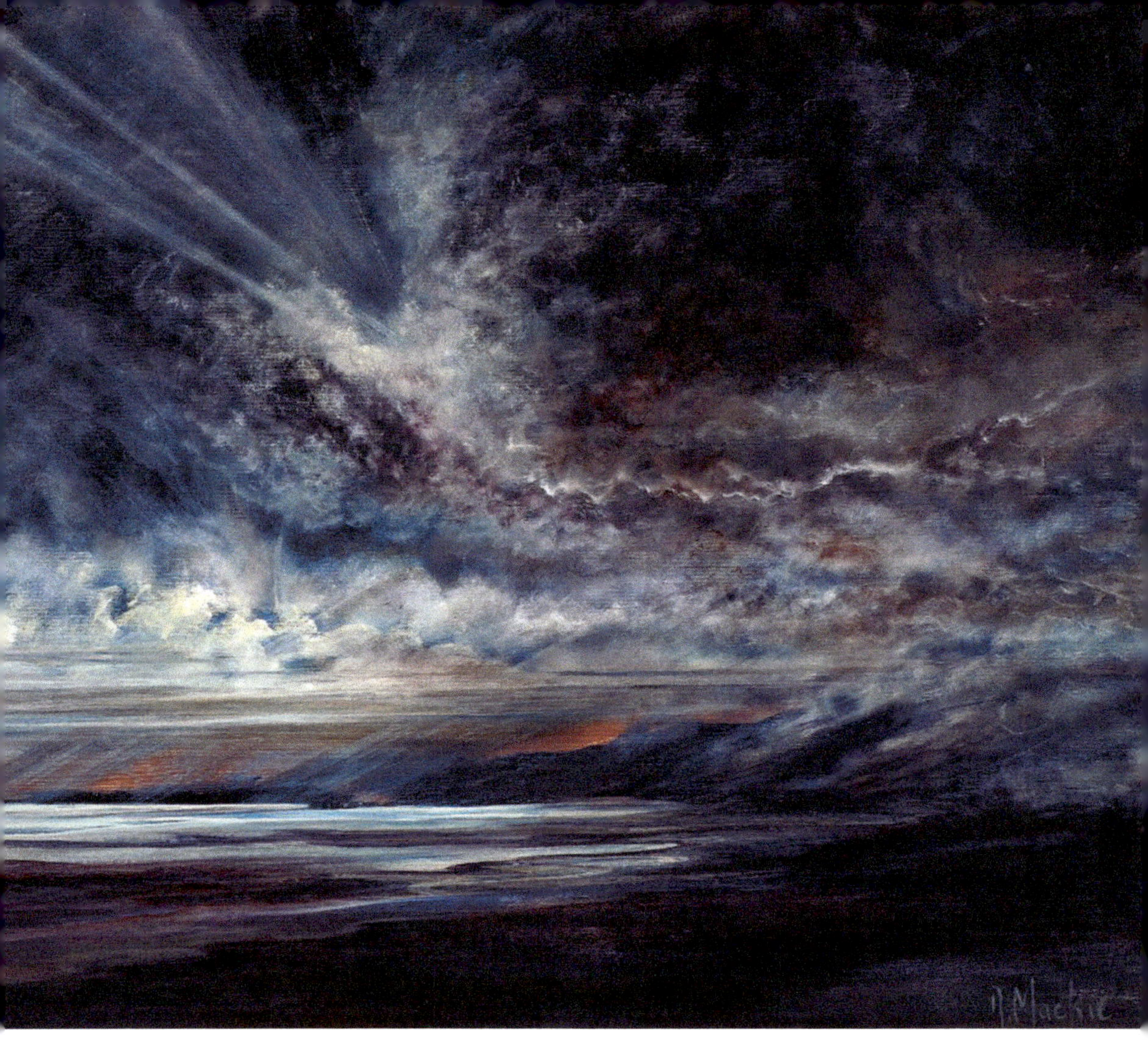

Dark Shoreline

Stein is on the Waternish Peninsula, which continues to Ardmore and the church at Trumpan. I left exposed the preparatory undercoat of light red to show the last of the sun's colours in the sky.

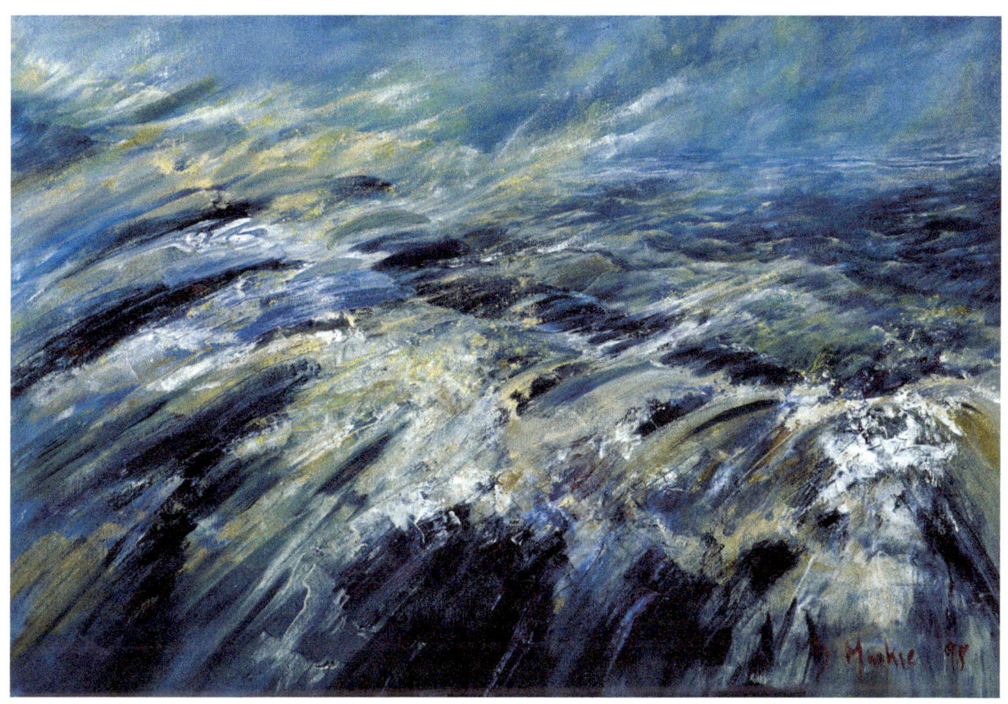

Force Ten

The power of the sea; skyline lost in a welter of spume.

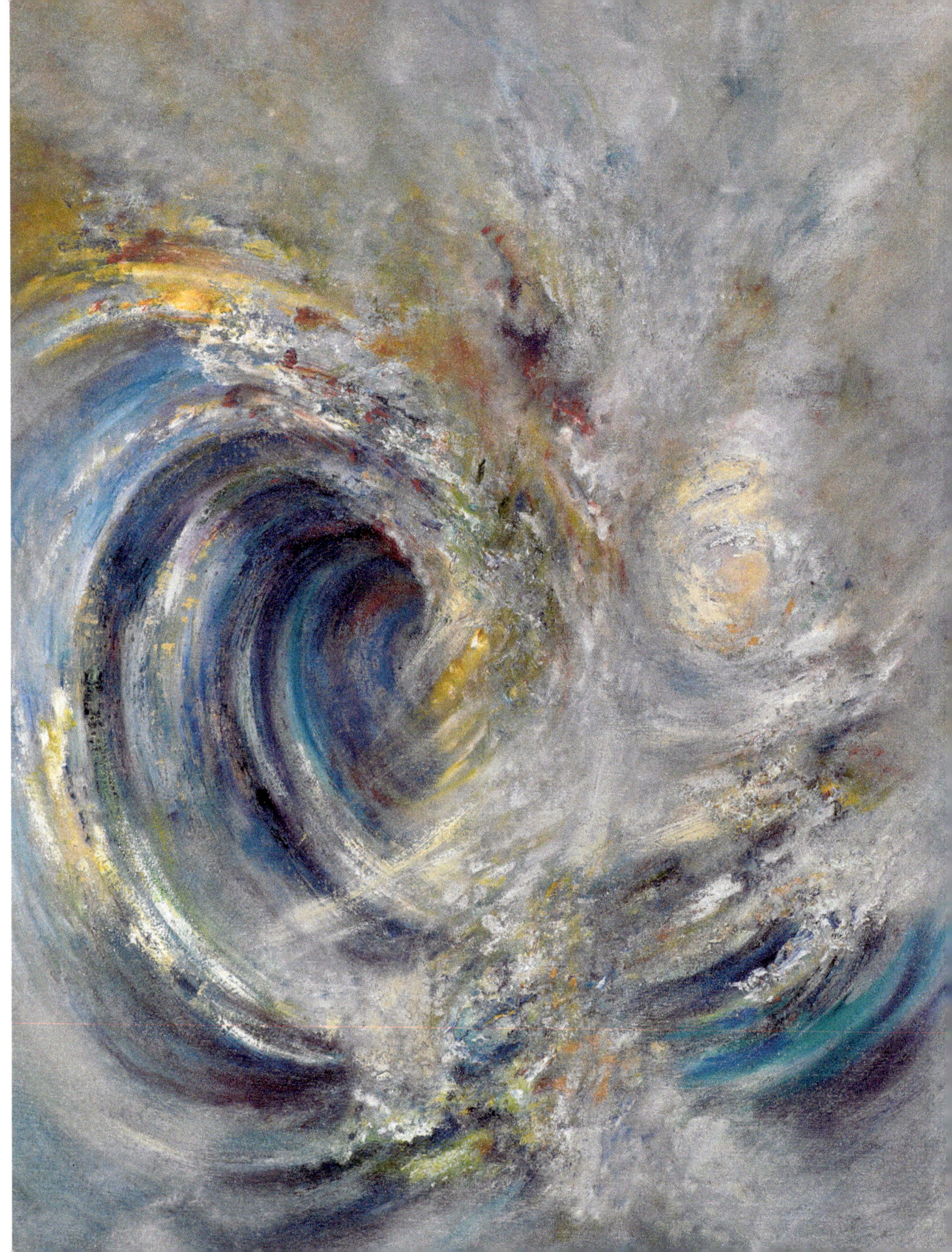

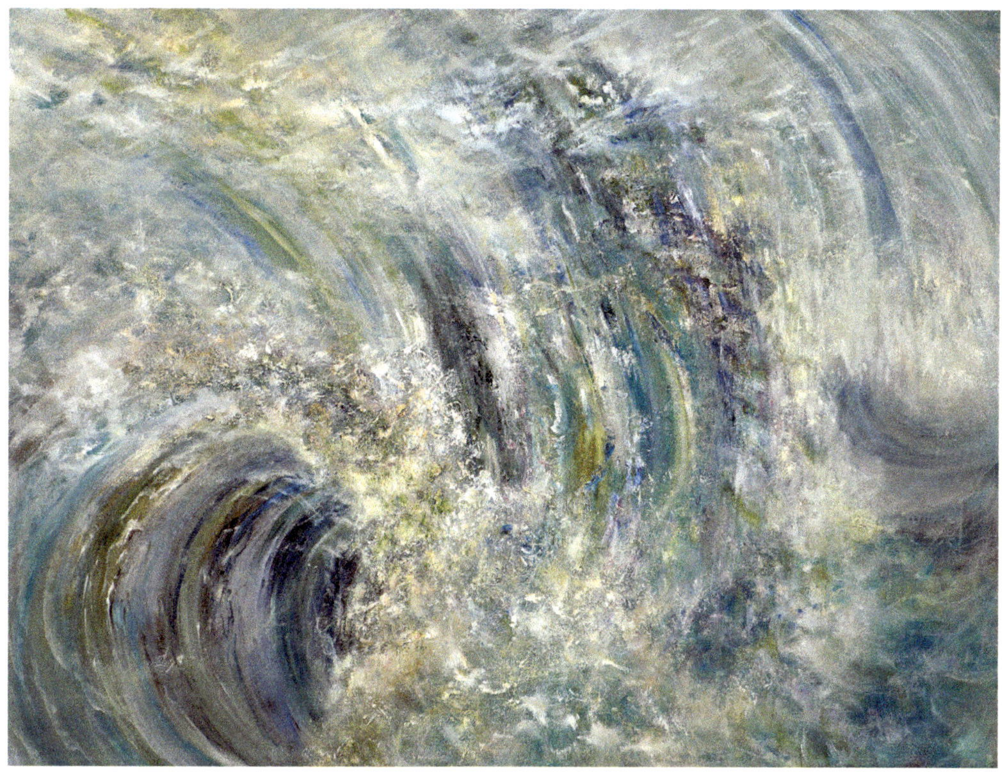

Inside the Wave (left)

Here I wanted to capture the ellipse of a wave's formation and a sense of proximity to the cylindrical tunnel. Taking an ellipse beyond the frame helps to convey this impression.

Turn of the Wave (above)

In essence the wave is clear water, but there are so many permutations of colour to be considered due to its reflective qualities and the accompanying movement as it breaks into a foaming state. I tried to keep a collective harmony of colour within the palette for this work.

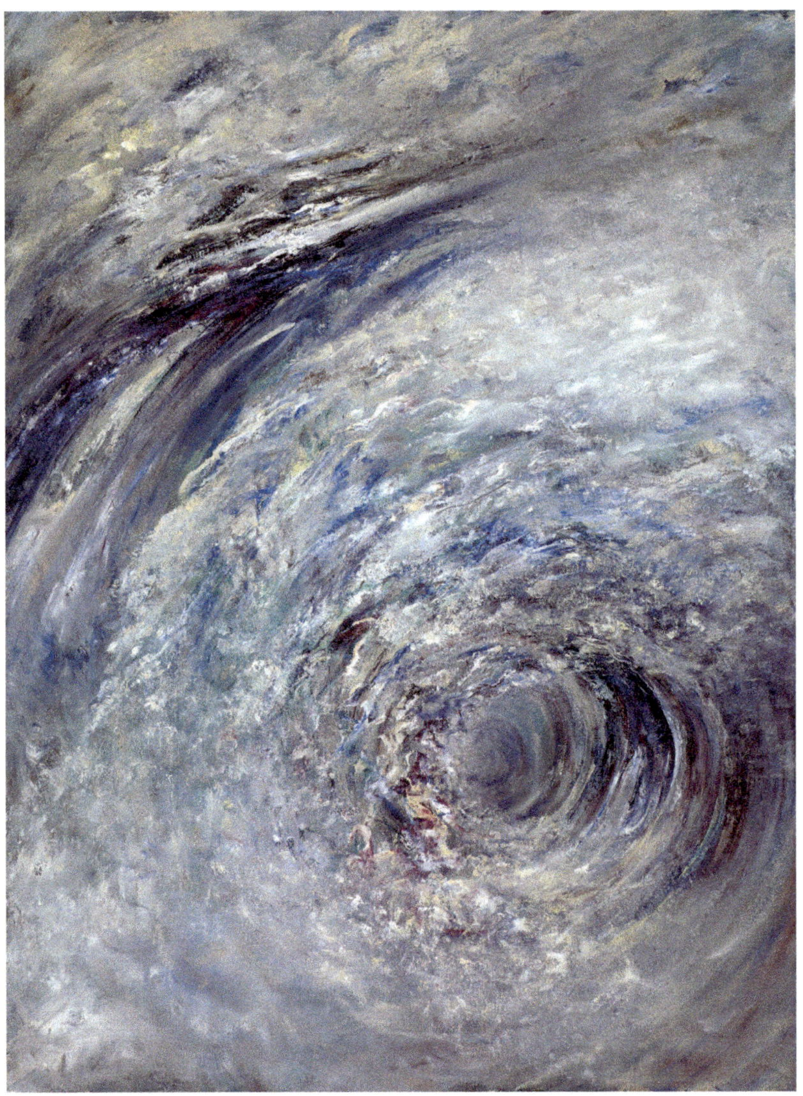

Surf Studies, 1 & 2

These large paintings dominated my studio for three months. They now hang
as a pair in a house in Cornwall which has breathtaking views of a wild sea.

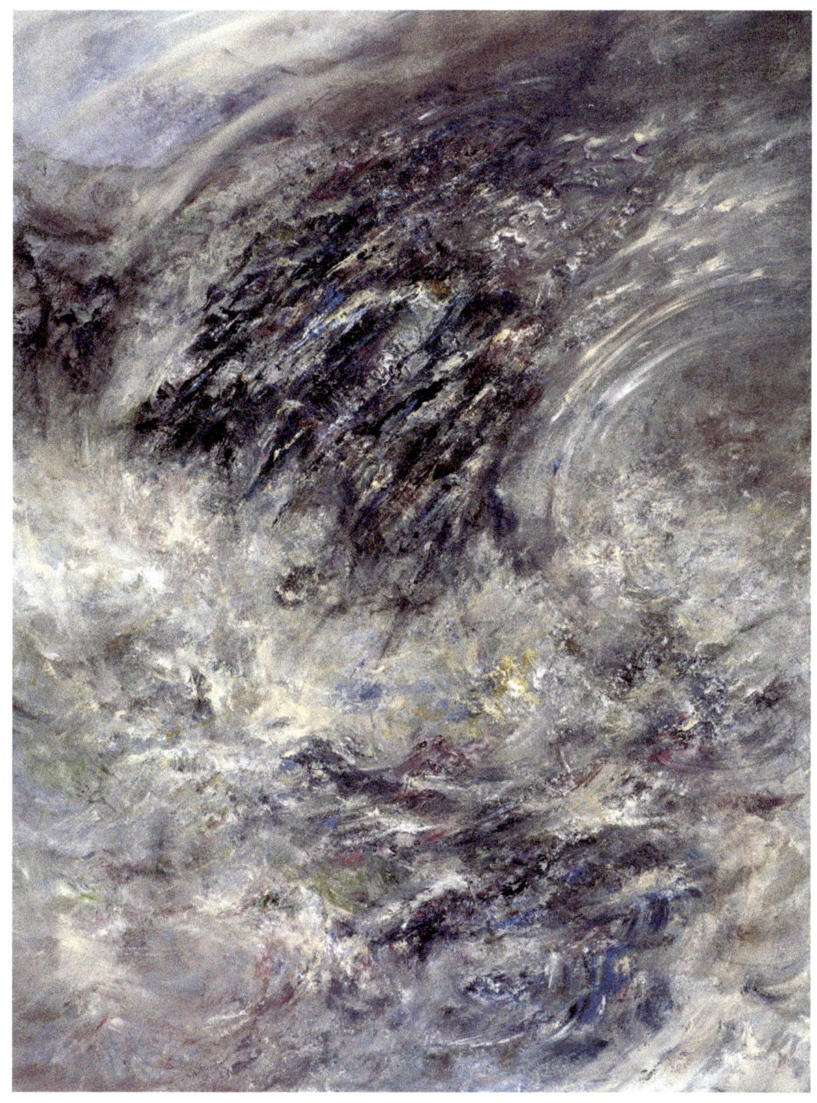

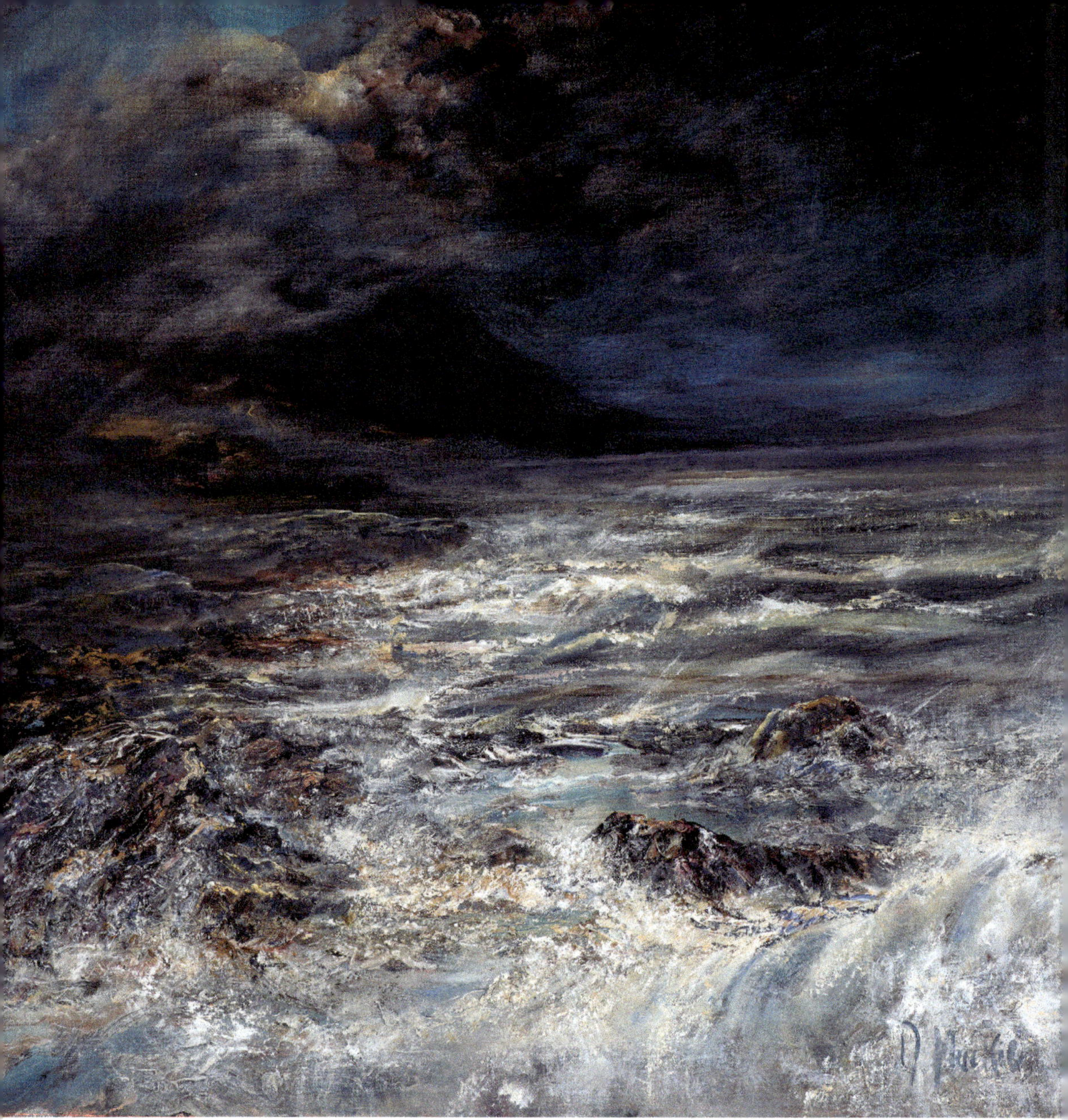

Stormy Coastline

A high tide, stormy, oppressive clouds and just a glimpse of sunshine –
a dramatic mix to challenge every element of my observational powers.

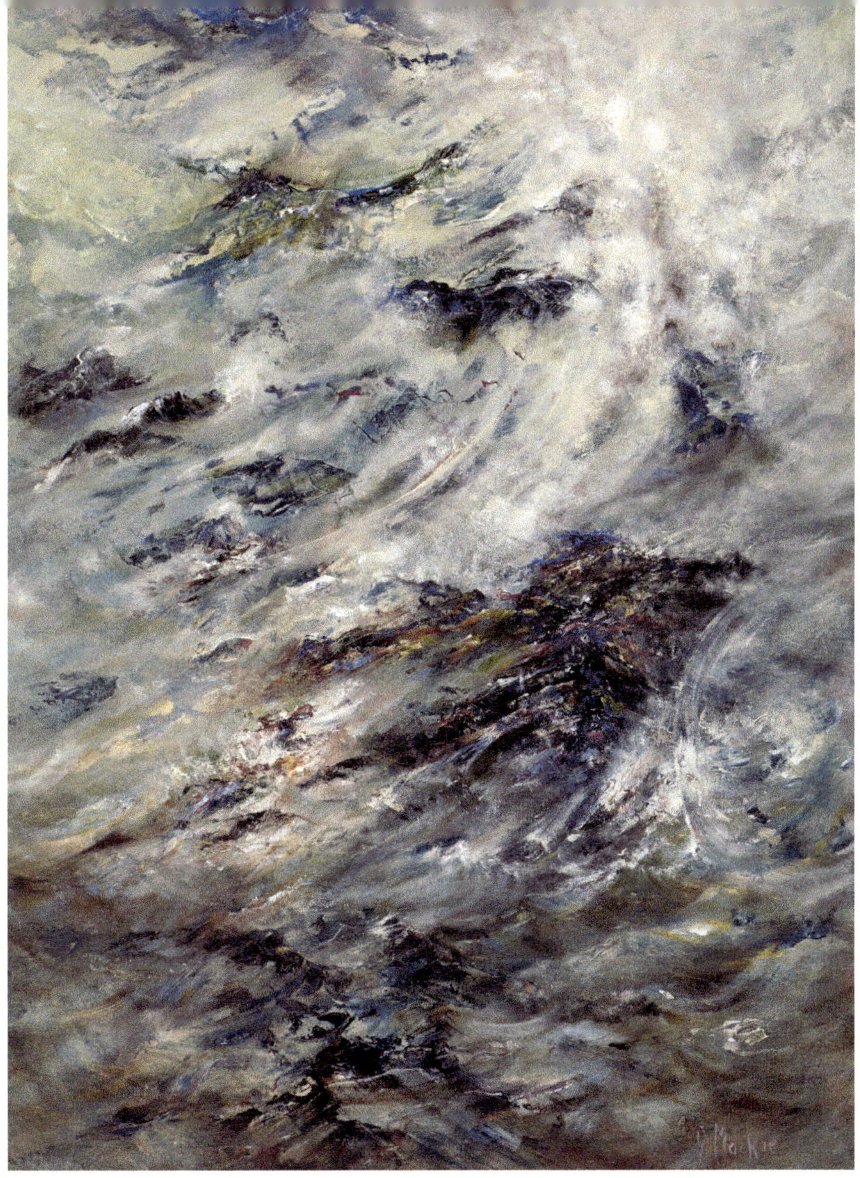

Looking Down on the Incoming Tide

Fisherman's Rock below the house at Borreraig is about 20ft high and
covered with turf. It is an ideal place to perch and watch the waves - so
many colours and shapes to be interpreted.

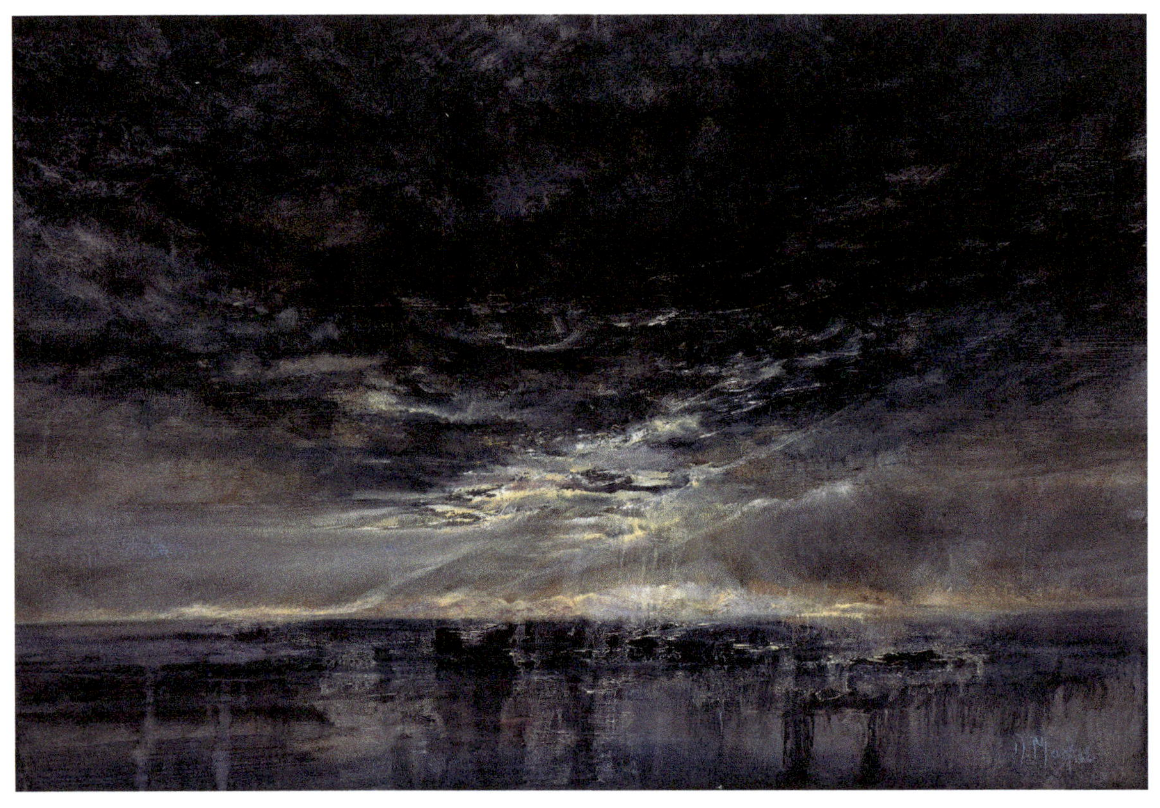

Light on the Outer Hebrides

Above the Minch an enormous dark cloud bank fans upwards and outwards, allowing the last rays of sunlight to fall across the Outer Hebrides. A watery turps wash gives the reflective surface of the sea greater credibility.

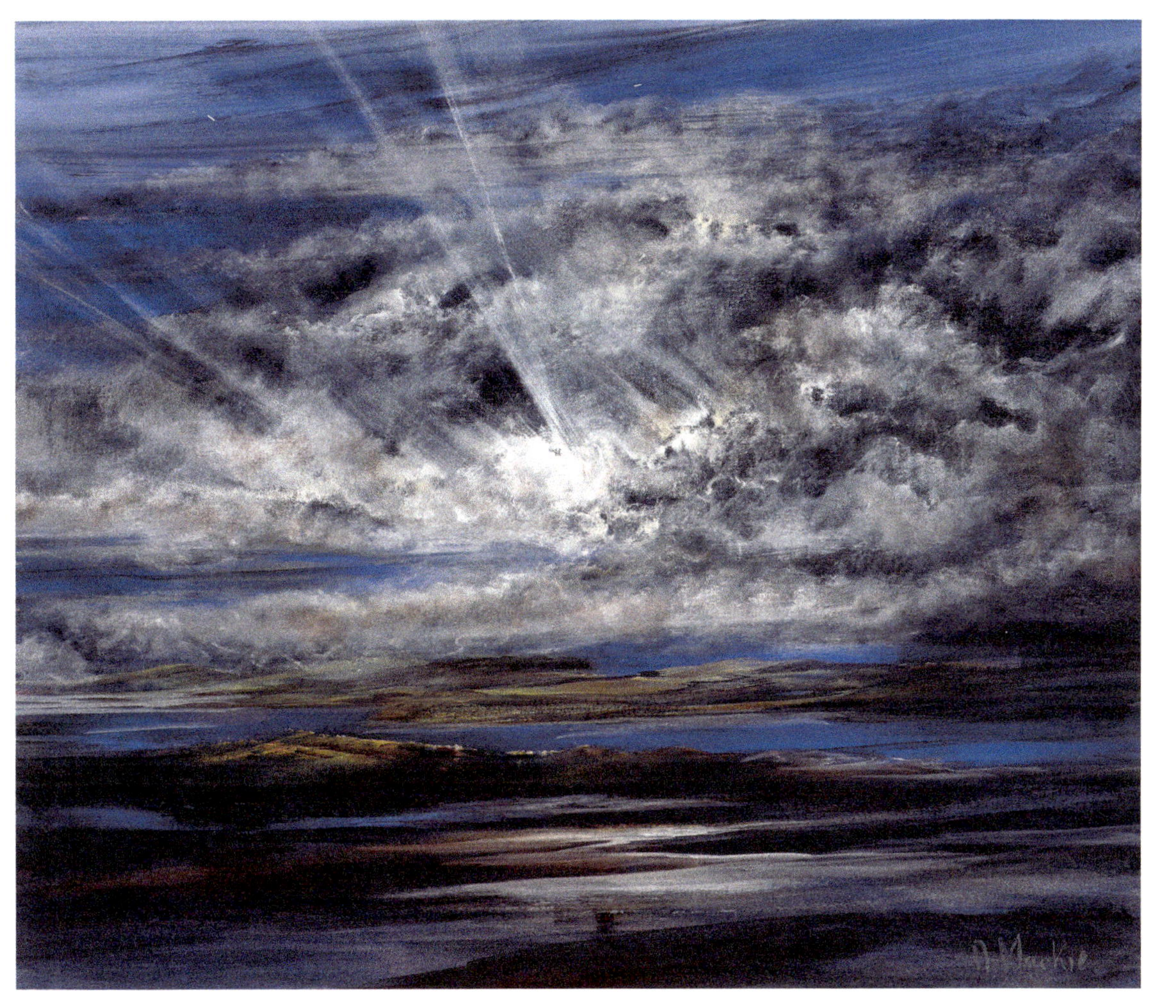

Evening, Low Tide

Driving from Sligachan to Sconser at low tide, I witnessed the charcoal clouds against an electric blue sky.

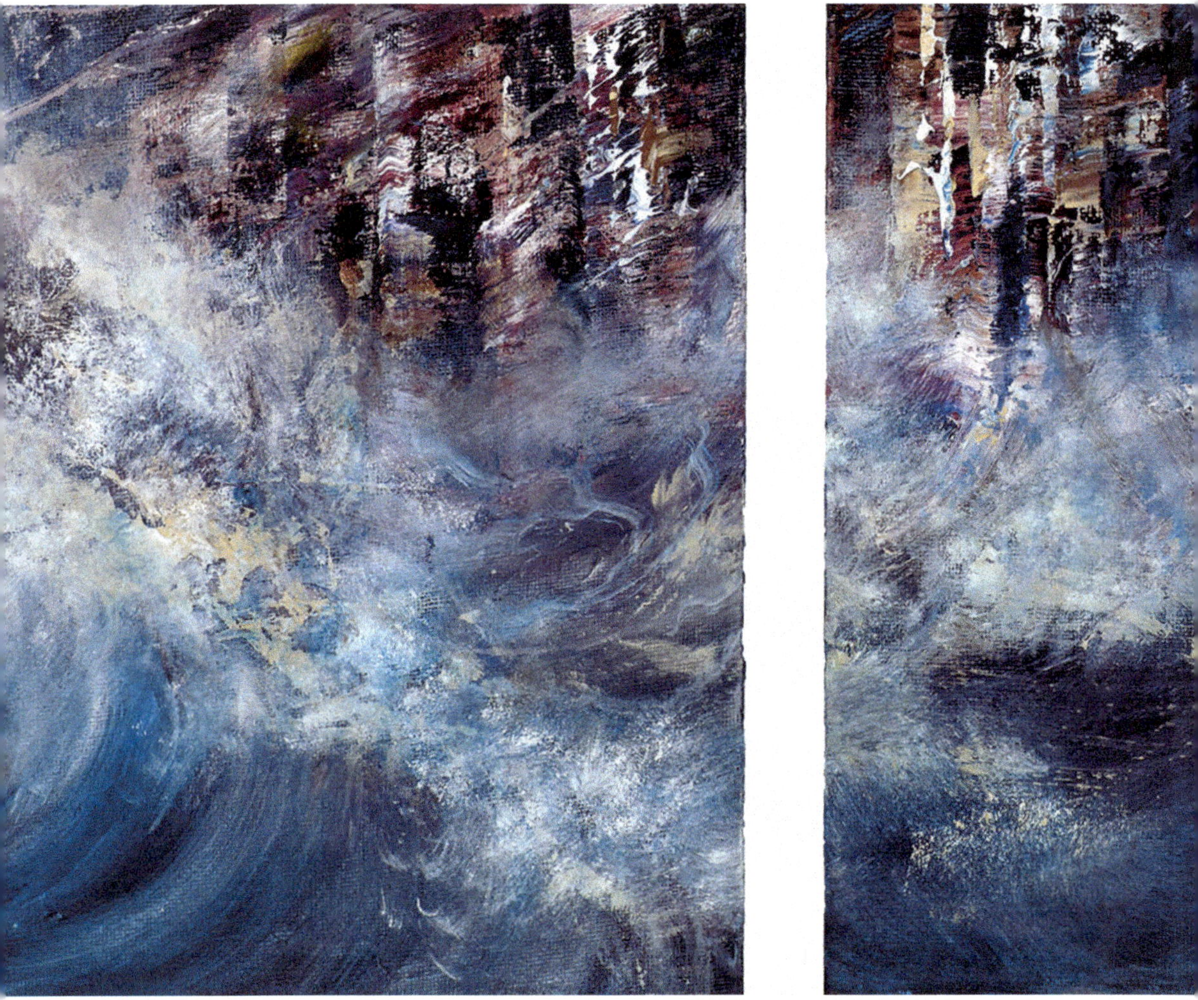

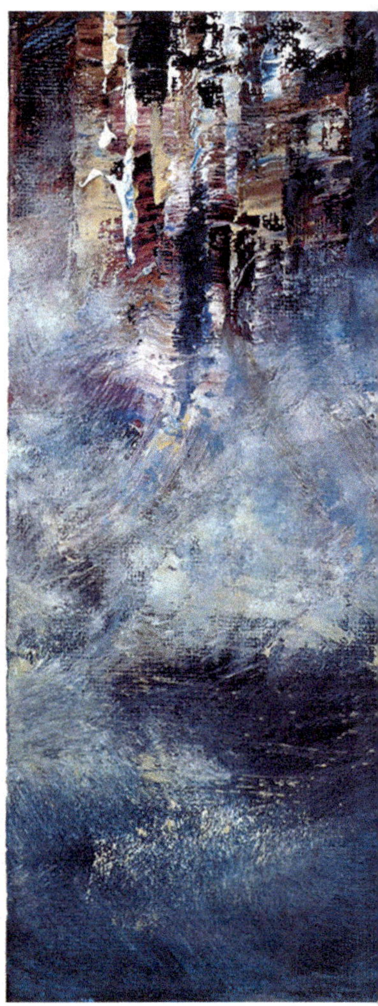

Rock Faces, triptych

The west coast of Scotland is renowned for its sailing. The experience varies depending on the weather and the size and handling of the boat. This particular evening, strong winds took us uncomfortably close to the rocks and you could say that this painting was brought about by fear. A triptych is used to optically extend the rock faces, which we were in danger of being dashed against.

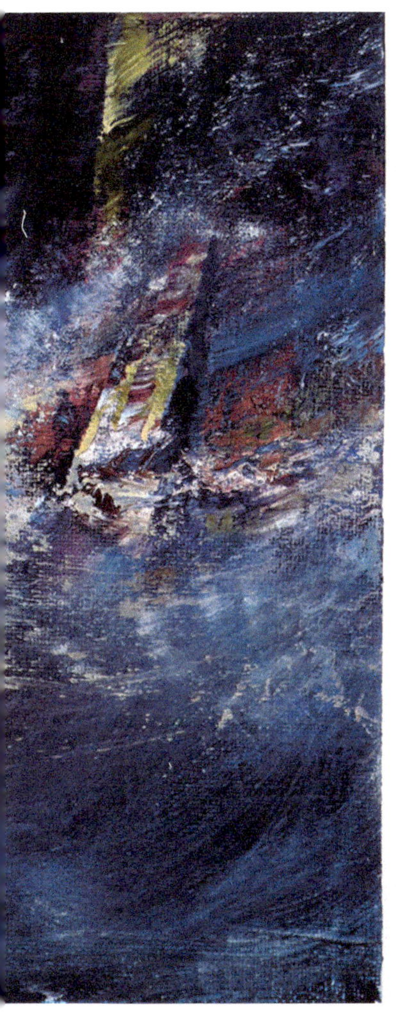

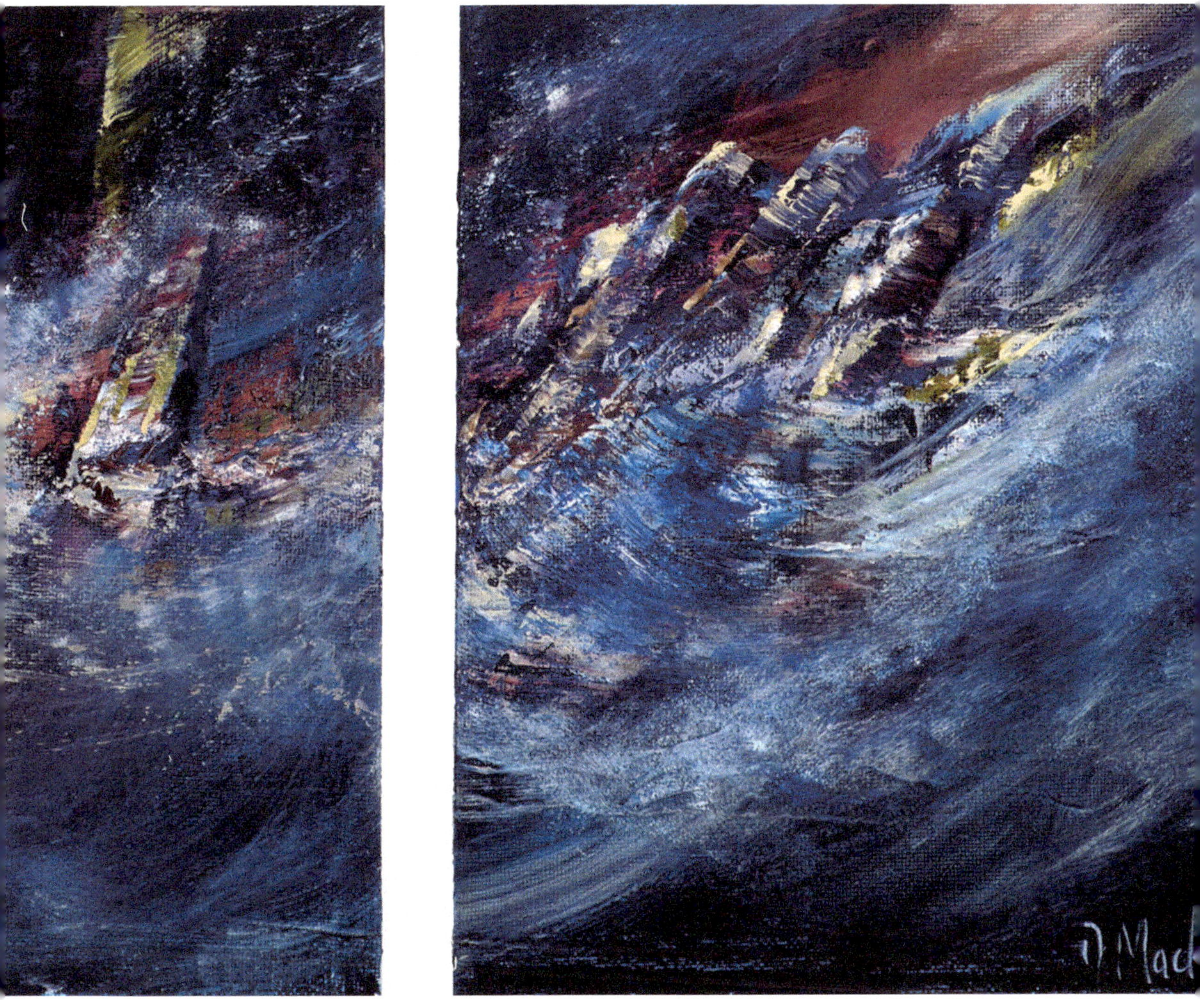

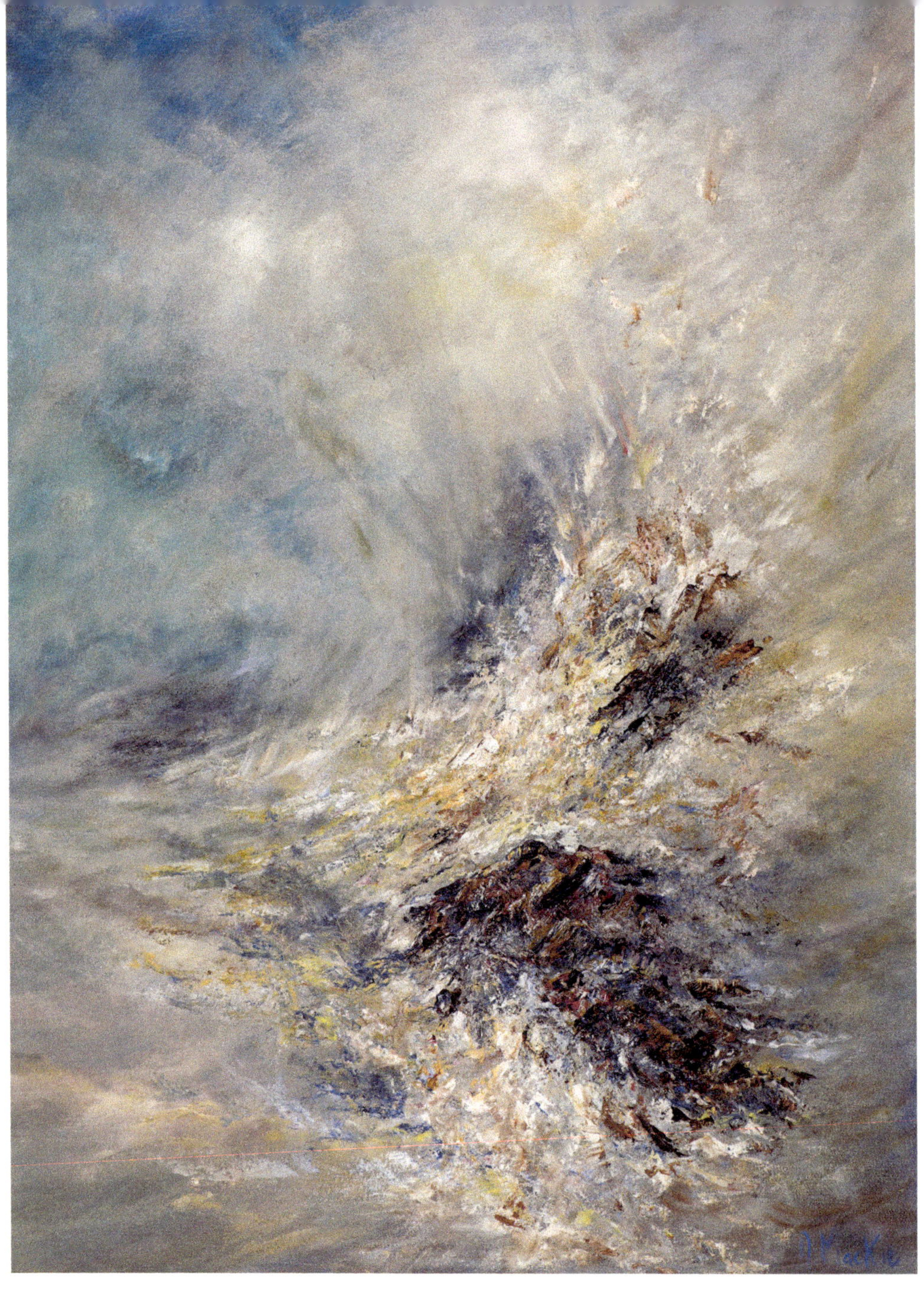

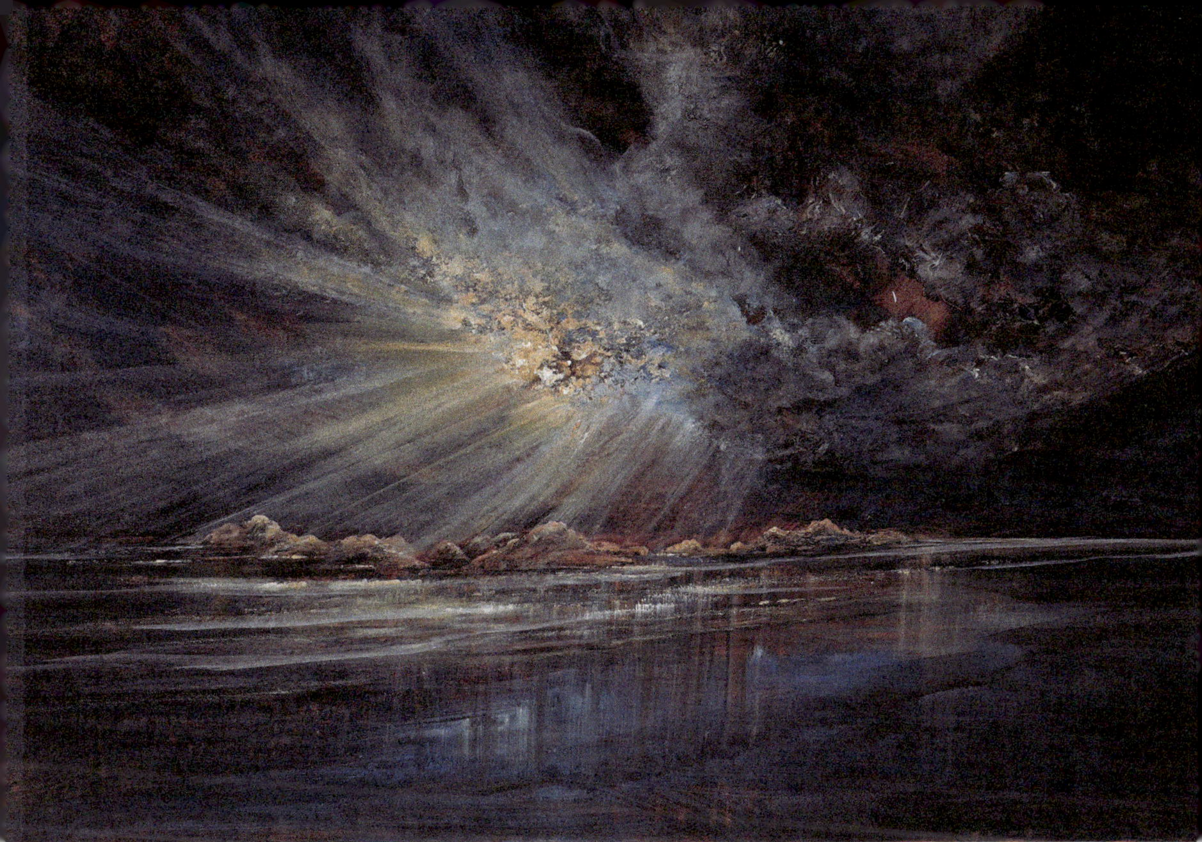

Autumn (above)

Looking across to Losaigh, Clett and Mingay, small islands in Dunvegan
Loch.

Waves and Rocks (left)

One of the best times to venture from the house to the shore is when the
weather is wild and windy. A small hide on the beach with a cosy stove
helps to keep out the winter chill and allows me all the time I need to watch
the myriad interactions of the waves as they impact on rocks and cliffs. If I
look hard and long enough, I seem to experience the scene in slow motion,
enabling me to separate the patterning from the point of impact to the
final, fan-like spray that dissipates into the atmosphere.

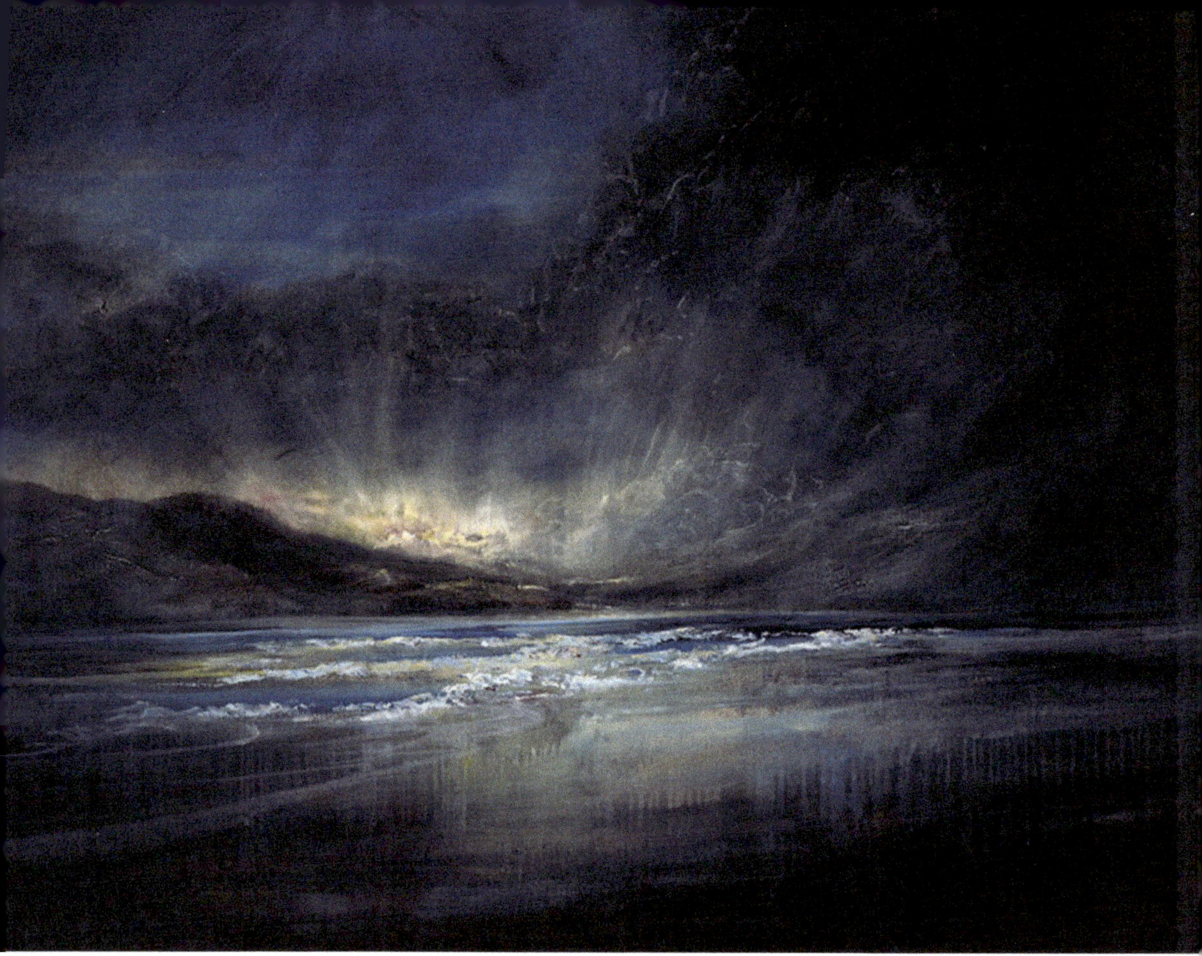

After the Sun

A wintry day on Talisker beach, where the sand is quite black but mixed with
fine broken shell. The waves breaking over the sand generate continually
changing patterns on its glass-like surface. To capture the power of the
scene, I took the risk of giving all the elements similar tonal values.

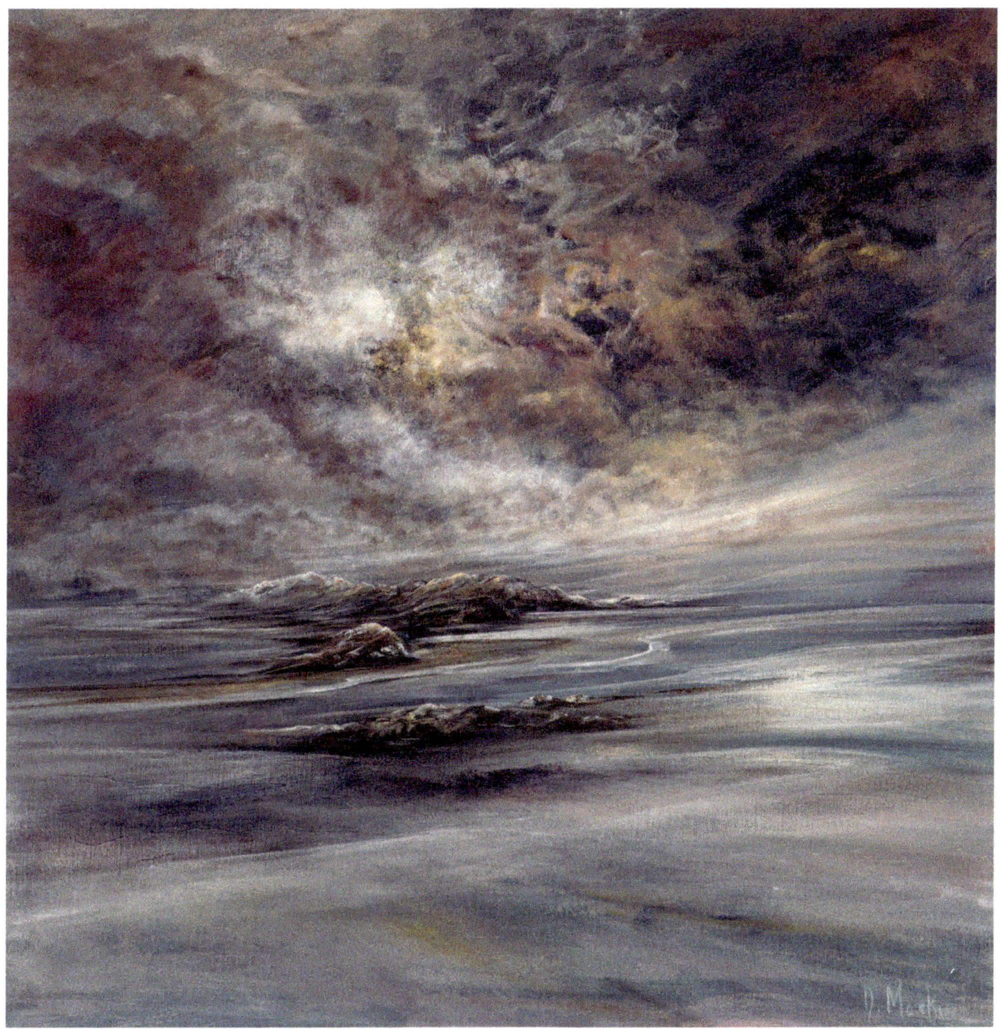

Tidal Islands

The stretch of road along the Waternish Peninsula towards Trumpan is
spectacular in all weathers. On this particular day, the sea was so calm I
felt it should be recorded, though it is normally wilder days that attract me.

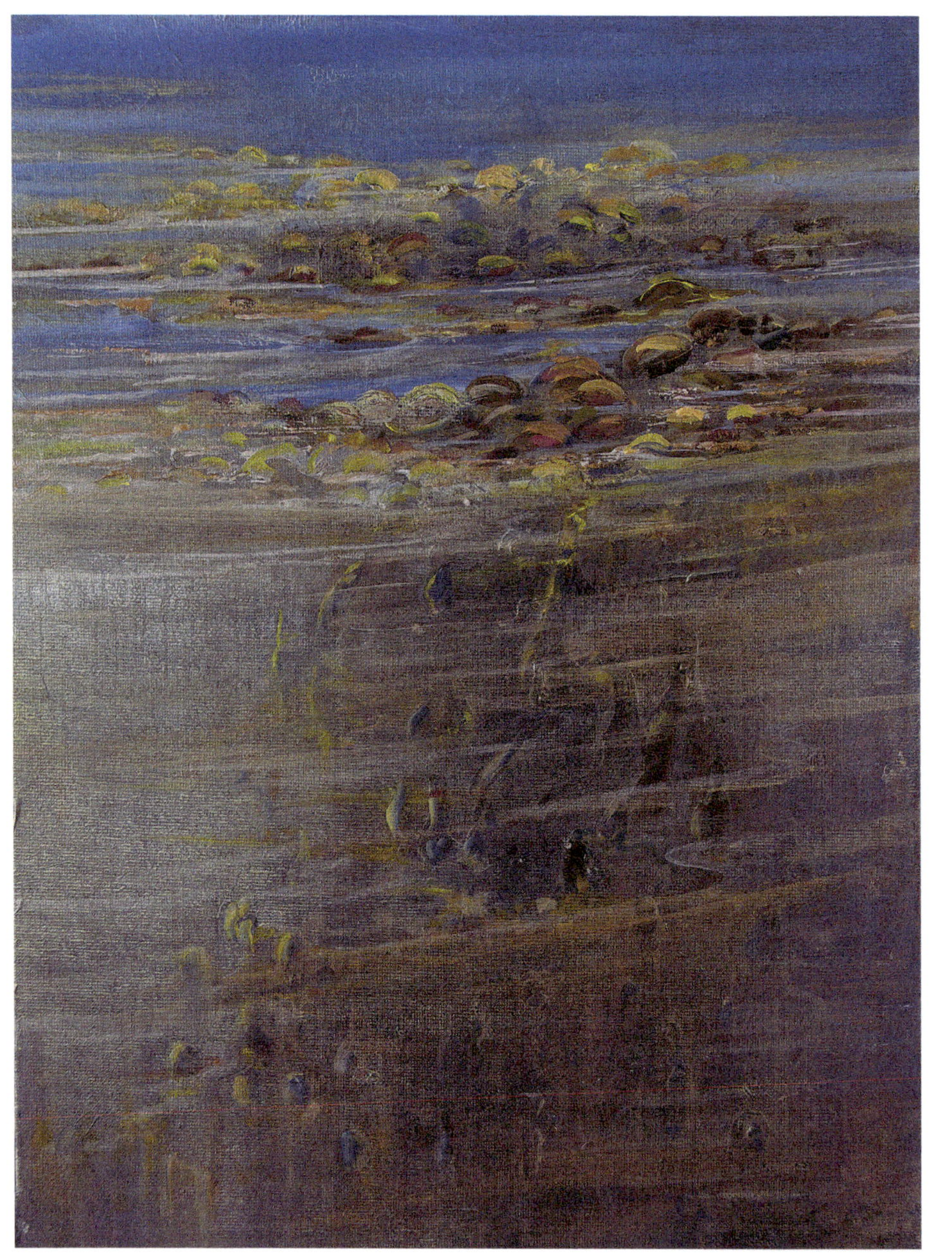

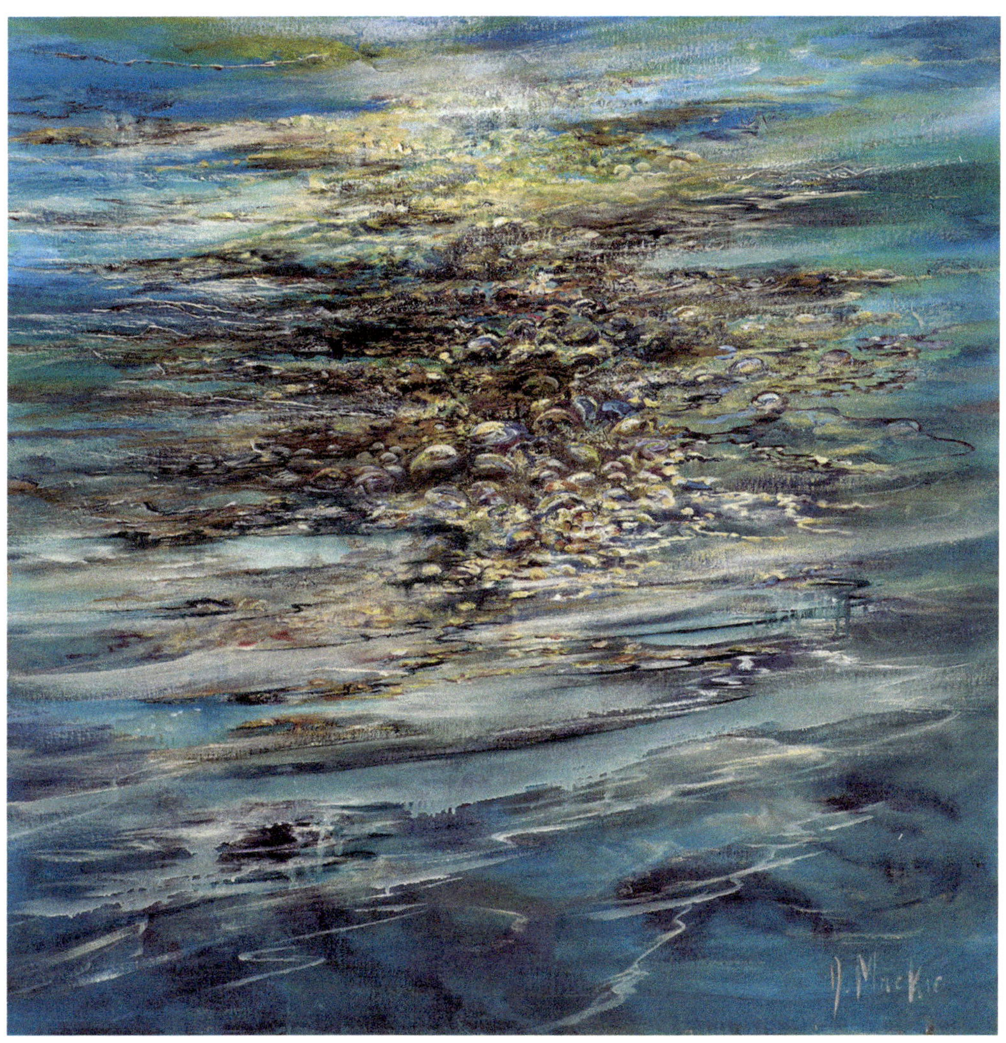

Seaweed Study (left)

Seaweed rising up from the seabed to lie glistening on the surface.

Bladderwrack in the Sunshine (above)

Bladderwrack floating, jewel-like, in the bright sunshine under a blue sky.

Early Morning Daisies

Daisies are wind resistant and their faces make beautiful moving shapes.

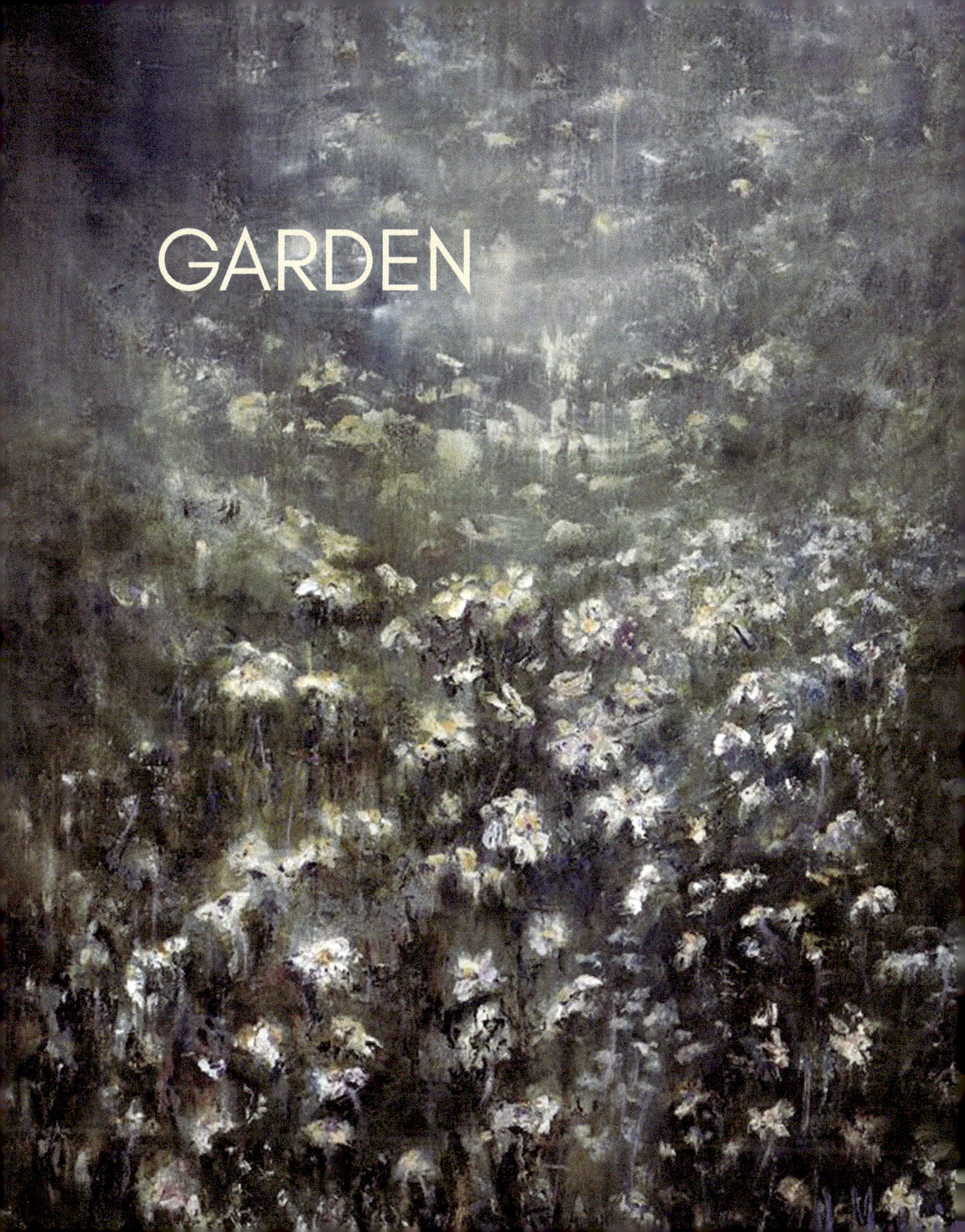
GARDEN

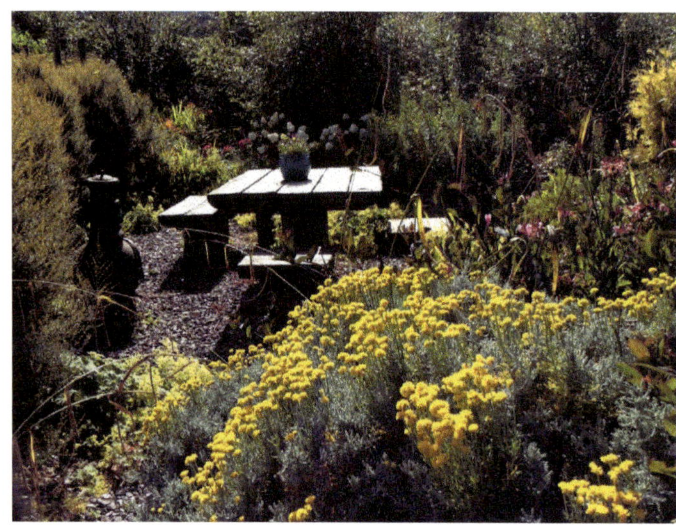

Left: A corner of the garden
Right: Steps to the beach

I HAVE HAD the great pleasure of making a garden out of a sheep field, which with its natural slopes progressing to the shore was a landscaper's dream. The big drawback is that we bear the brunt of the northerly gales and the prevailing westerly winds have blown many an optimistically planted shrub clean out of the ground. My first task was therefore to create some sort of shelter belt that would allow new plantings some degree of protection.

At the outset, I was wisely advised to take a good look around the local area to see what was thriving. It is always such a temptation to buy something glorious in the garden centre, only to see it suffer and die in the wrong conditions.

Any sort of boundary can be stark when a garden is threading its way through open countryside. The old stone walls that separate the fields around our house are gradually being supplemented with wire sheep fencing. I decided to mirror this by using wire fencing for the outer boundary of the garden, and then within three metres of that we built a dry stone wall that looks partially collapsed as it curves its way gently down the grassed slope to join the path to the shore. The planting between the stone wall and the wire fence is a collection of birch, fuschia, elaeagnus and white *Rosa rugosa*, so there is a good mix

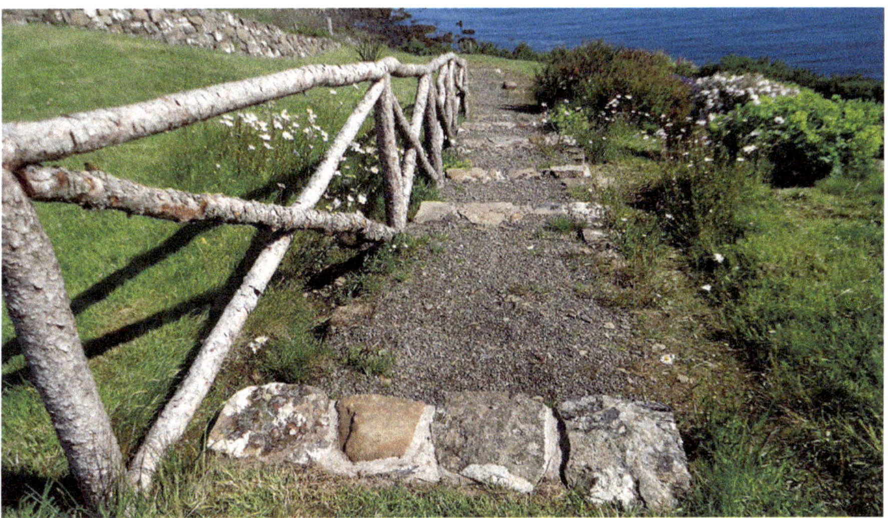

of deciduous and evergreen planting; the hips from the *Rosa rugosa* bushes make a welcome addition to the birds' diet. Oxeye daisies and chamomile are firm favourites of mine. Over time, from one seed packet, I have established them on the banks and beside pathways down to the shore. The oxeye daisy is particularly wind resistant and *en masse* they move so beautifully together.

I wanted to transform an area of the garden on the cliff edge that was densely covered with waist-high bracken, where I was keen to have a seating area. I also had the idea of digging out around the waterfall that falls to the beach below. It was time

to bring a digger in! I find it beyond exciting to see these mechanised earth movers at work shaping the land. A level area for a table and benches was established. Rough timbers were cut into lengths at a local sawmill to provide a table and benches that could be cemented into the ground – there is no point in thinking that even heavy garden furniture will stay put here in the gales, so cement is the best solution.

The last task was to stop anyone going over the edge of the cliff, but I did not want a fence of any sort and so I decided on a double planting of gorse. Cut to a height of about a metre, the thickly prickled hedge

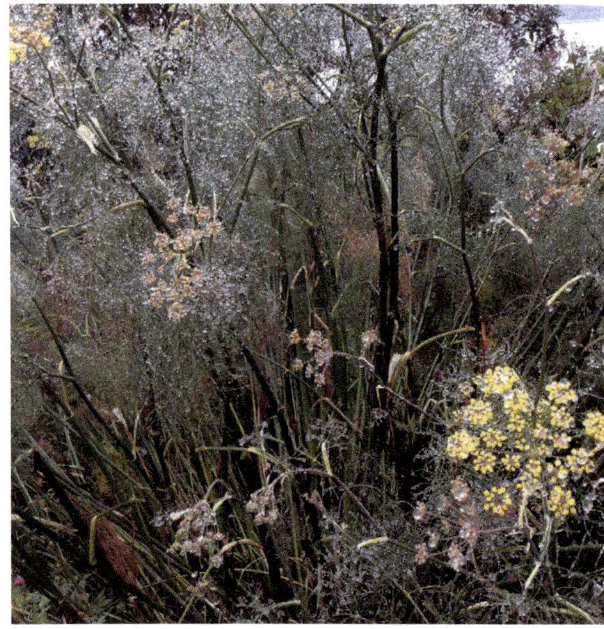

Fennel

is more than a deterrent, without compromising the site or obstructing the view in any way.

The waterfall running down the cliff below was originally almost covered with weeds, shrubs and wind-torn trees, the majority of which we managed to remove. I have planted white and red fuchsias so that the dancing blooms accompany the water as it descends from cliff to shore.

I have had some success growing cabbages in my vegetable patch. Watching their development through to maturity intrigues me. I find them so beautiful first thing in the morning, droplets of moisture sitting like cabochon stones on their leaves. Skye storyteller George Macpherson tells the tale of the magnificent cabbages of Glendale, said to have grown some 6ft across in days gone by. The story goes that, along with a few survivors, cabbage seeds were retrieved from the wreck of a Spanish galleon. The walled areas where these seeds were originally planted can still be seen in Glendale. With the success of the crop, trade developed between Skye and Ireland, exchanging cabbages for potatoes.

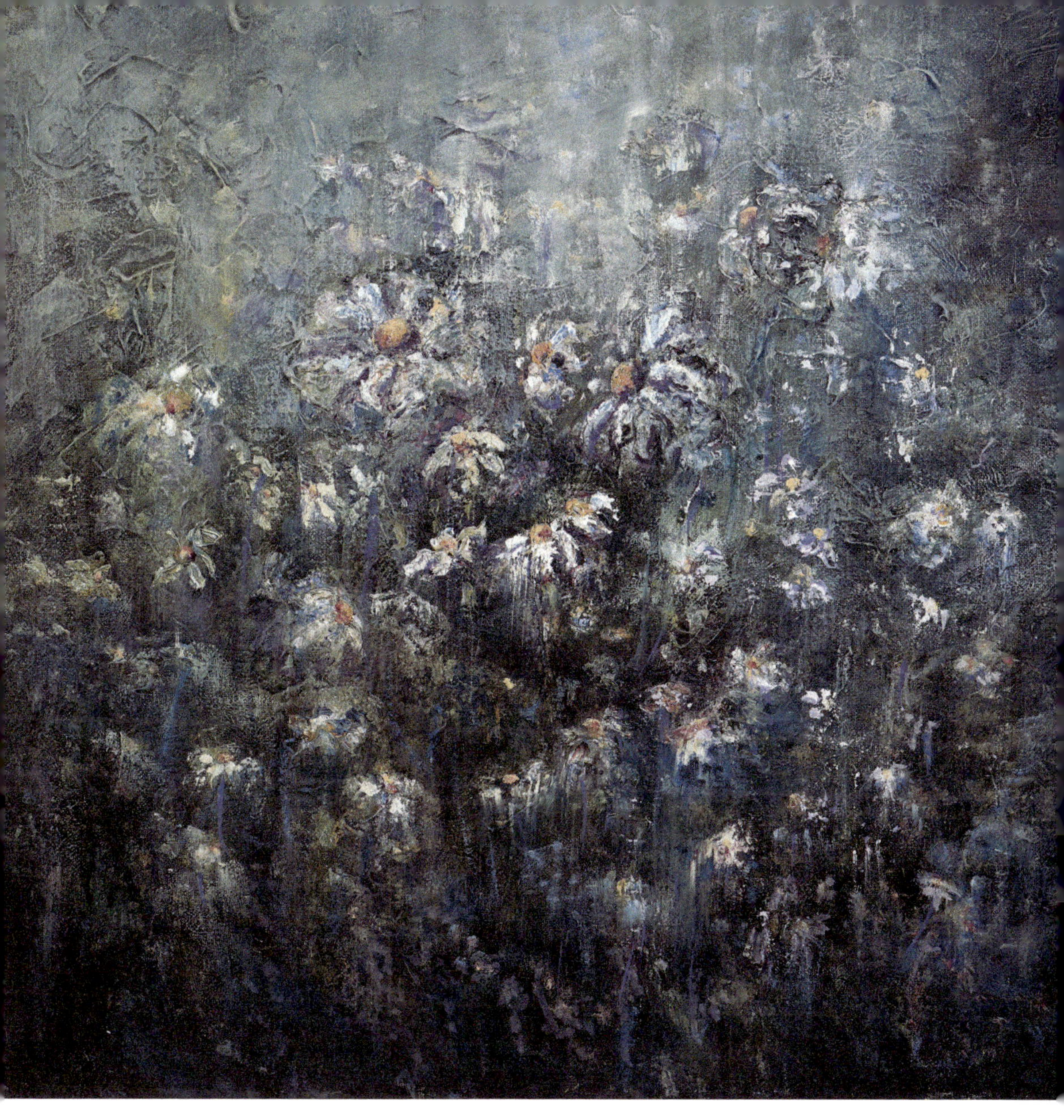

Daisies, a Closer Look
Daisies, from bud form to fully petalled.

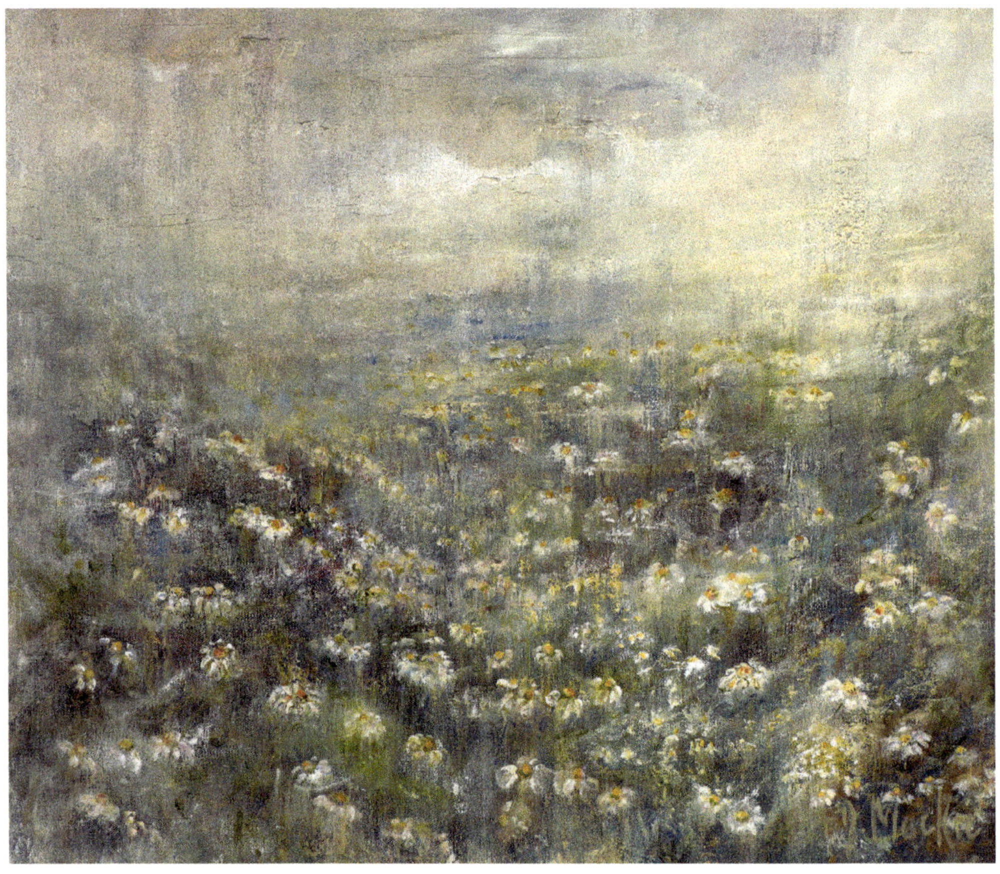

Early Morning Daisies (above)

On a misty morning at first light, daisy heads seem to float above the
ground.

Cabbage Portrait (right)

The challenge was to understand and represent the surface and structure
of the leaves, showing how they form in relationship with one another.

Cabbage (overleaf)

So many unexpected colours collectively produce a viable cabbage plant.

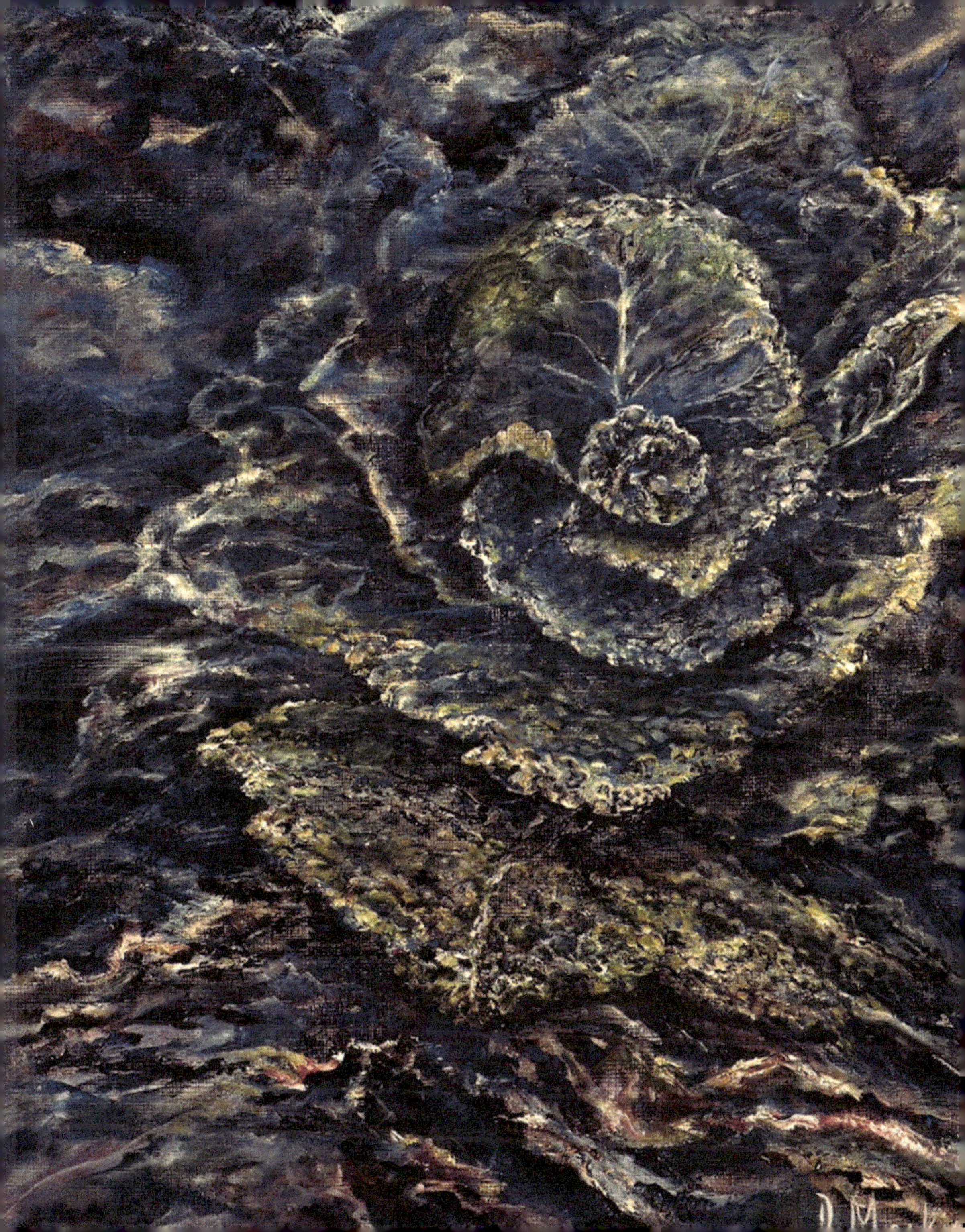

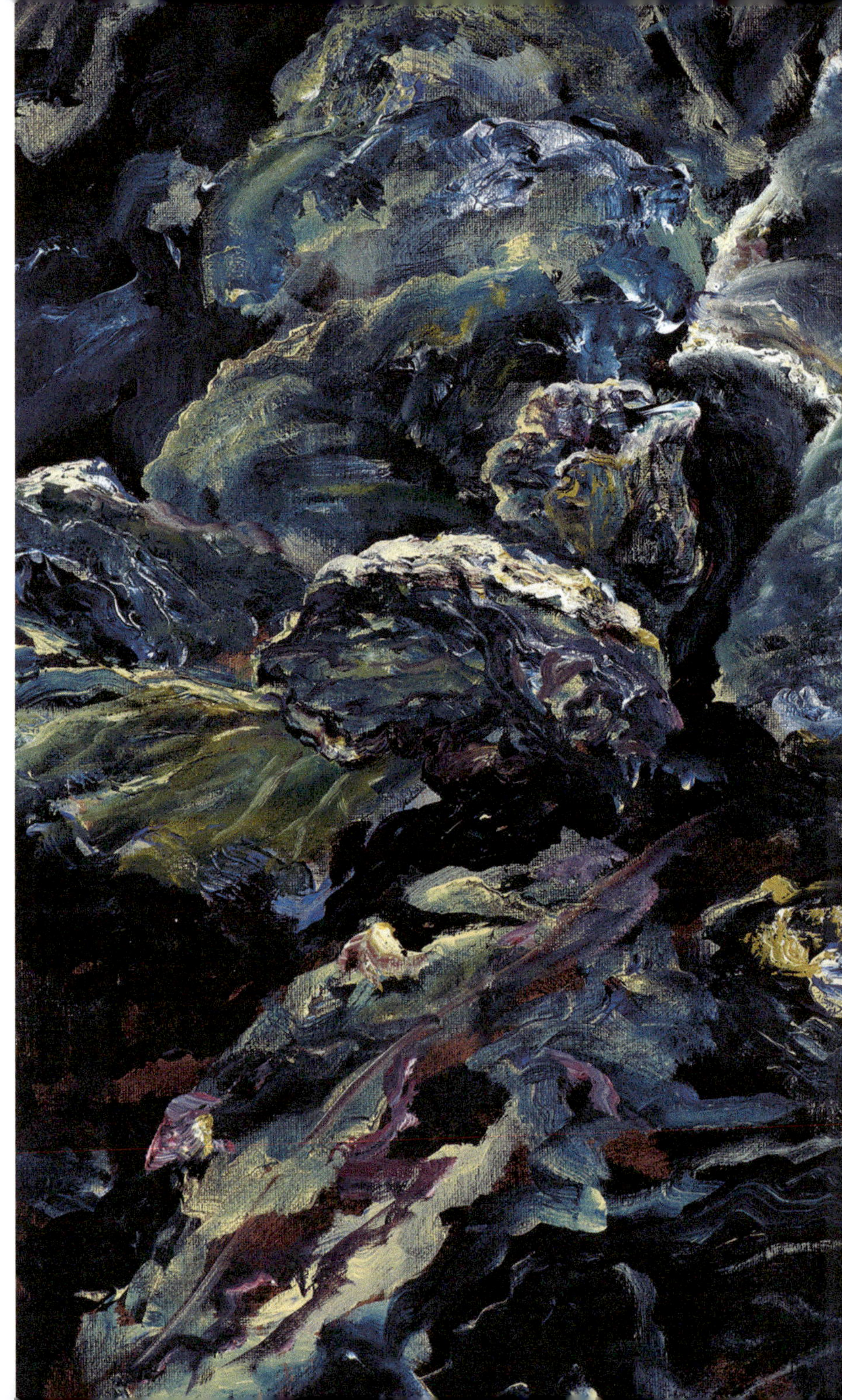

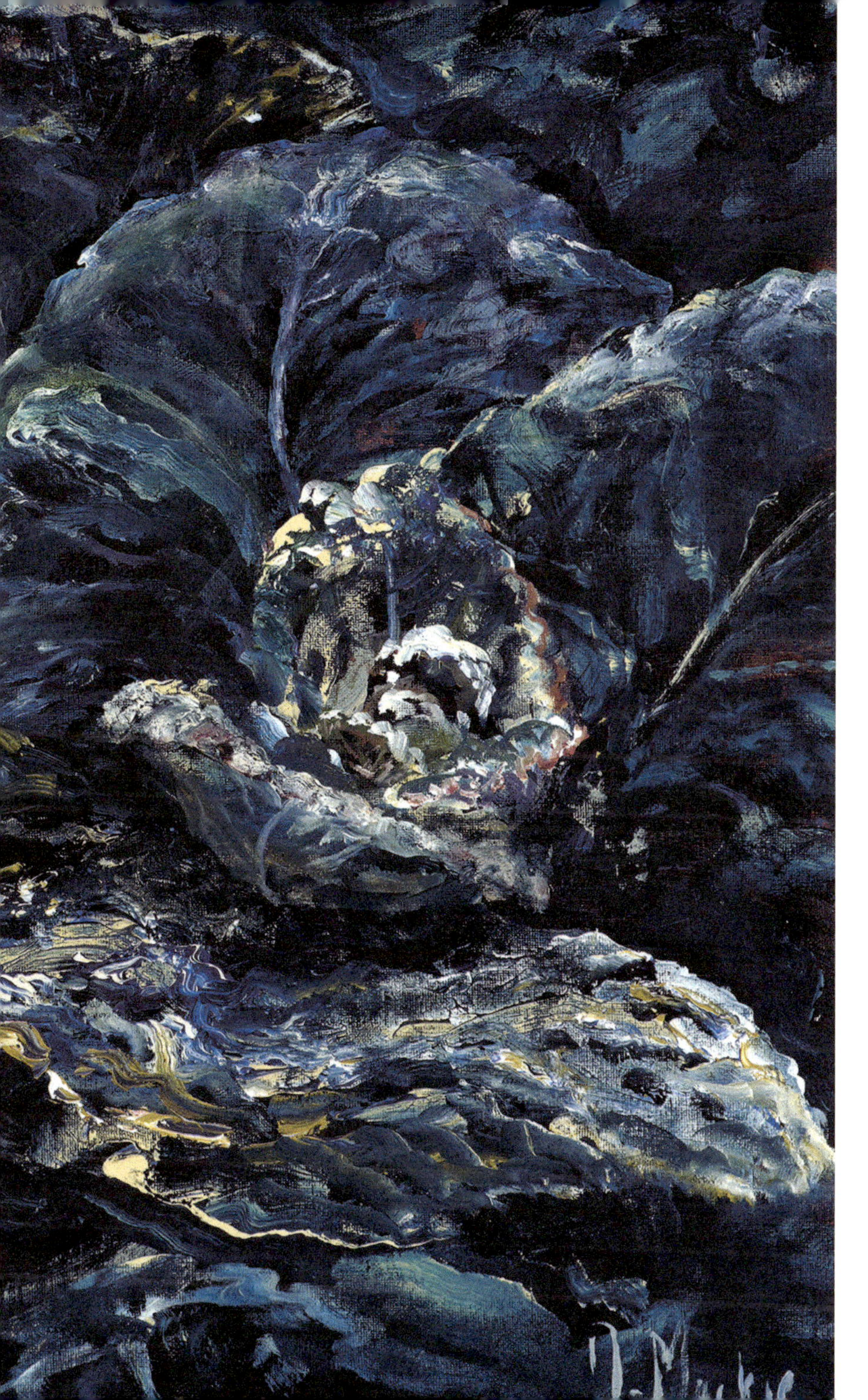

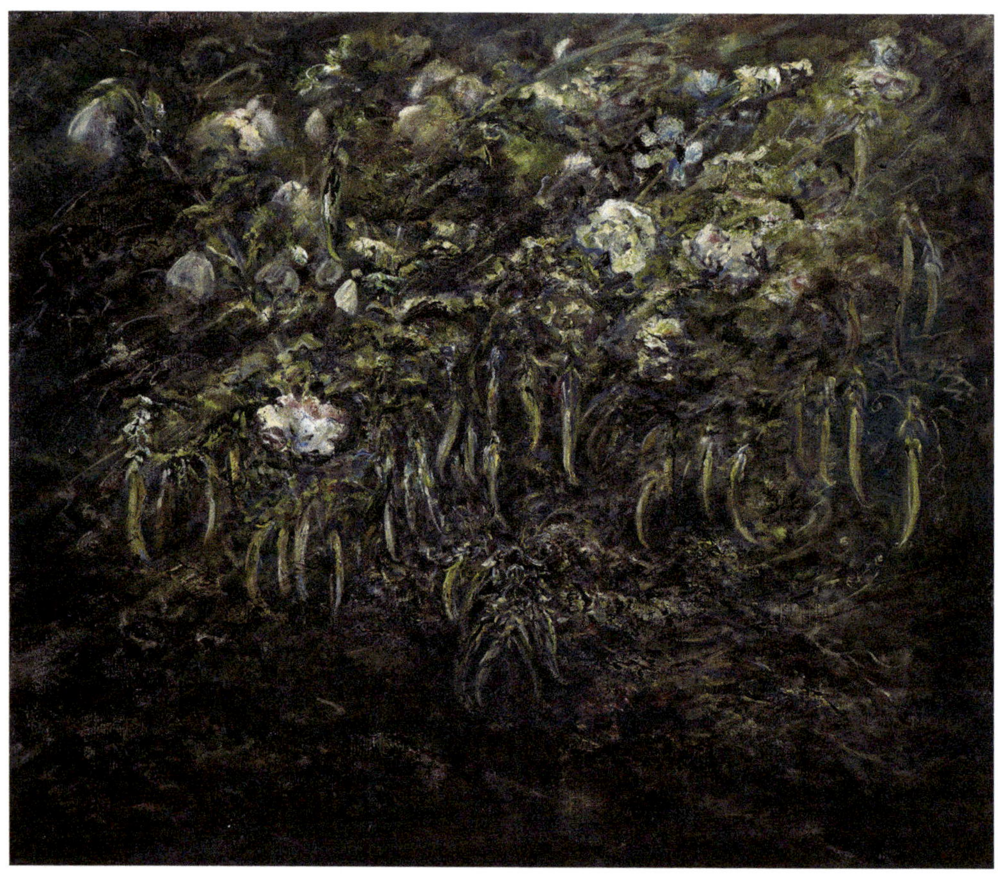

Peas (above)

Daunted by the complexity of the pea plants growing in the garden,
I resorted to draping a bundle around the easel for close examination.

Rhubarb (right)

Rhubarb is a plant that takes me back to my childhood, imagining its
umbrella leaves offering shelter to the fairy folk, bugs and tiny mammals.
Munching on a bright pink stalk covered in caster sugar was such a treat.

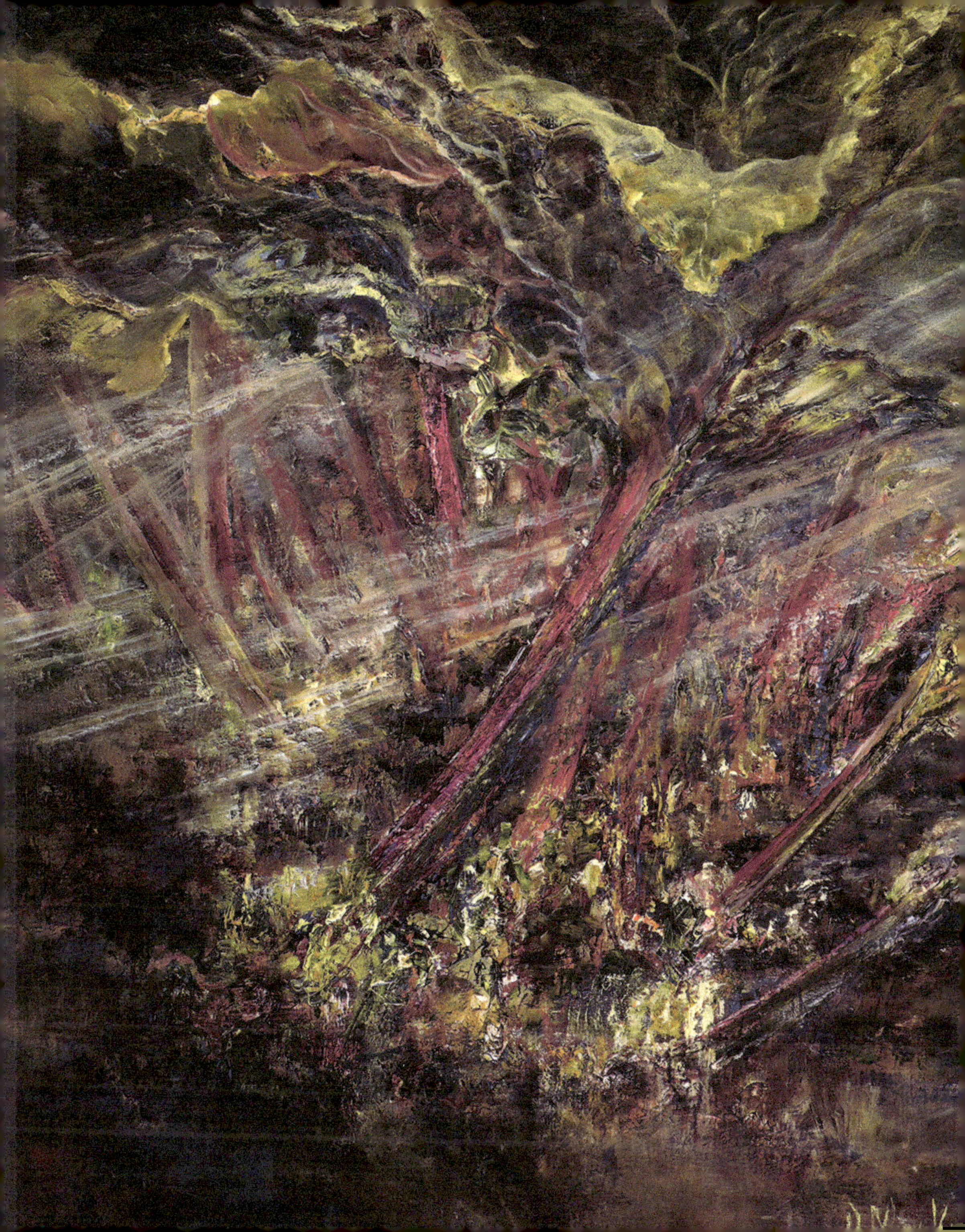

Woodland, Carbost

A rocky hillside covered with moss and lichen reveals its primroses before
the hazel trees regain their foliage.

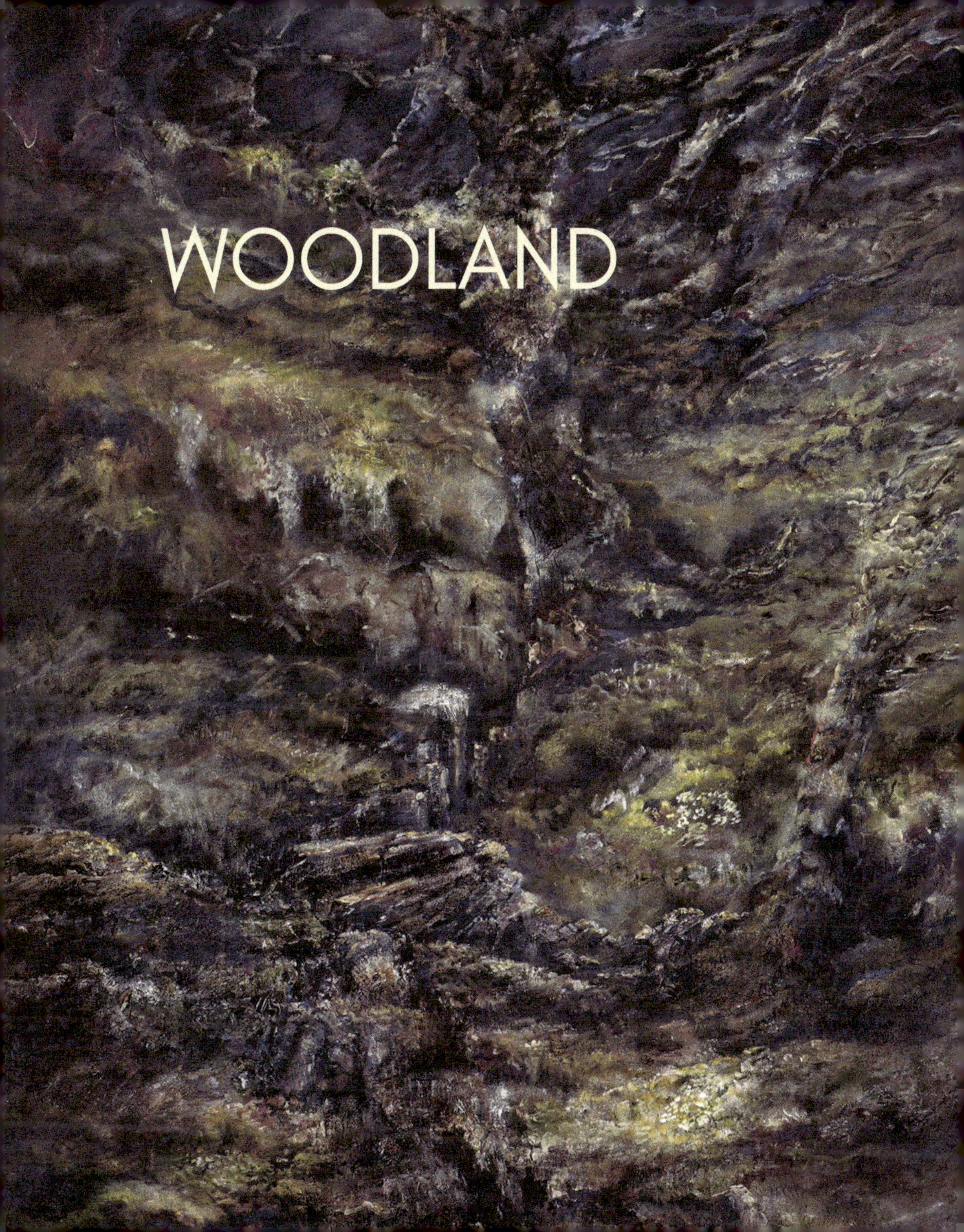
WOODLAND

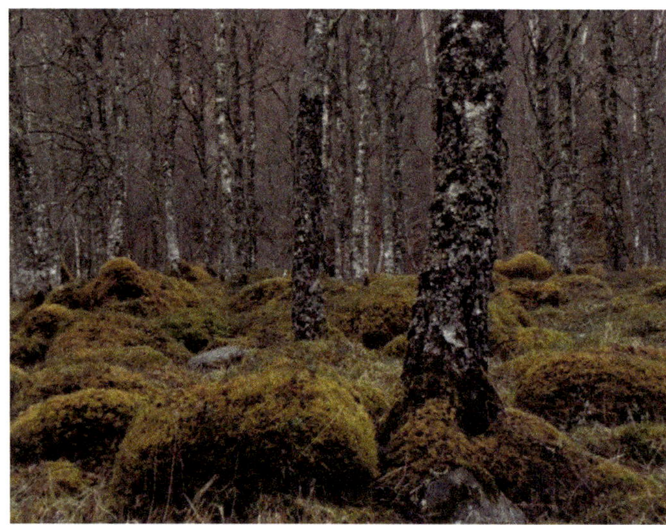

Mossed Boulders

ONE OF MY favourite woodland areas on Skye is near Dunvegan Castle. Around the village of Dunvegan there are undulating hillsides of established and newly planted trees. Once within the wood, I find that my senses are immediately heightened. The ground is covered with mossy boulders and a variety of ferns flourish in the low light. When the ferns first unroll their fronds, they bring a sense of the earliest form of plant life.

The narrow path goes through rhododendron, ash, birch, larch and fir. Larch offers bright bursts of lime green needles in spring, and in the autumn, glorious rust-coloured needles accompanying tiny cones.

For me, an enjoyable aspect of these woods is their strong legacy of Victorian planting. About half a mile up the steepening track, the remains of an old iron gate mark a boundary of bygone days; huge monkey puzzle trees have been planted here, some now sadly broken by the gales.

The path then continues across the moor to meet the Portree Road, from which, looking back towards the coast, you can see the various impacts of woodland management, from logging to replanting.

I like to walk back through a cut-off that takes me down to a burn. It feels so secretive and secluded

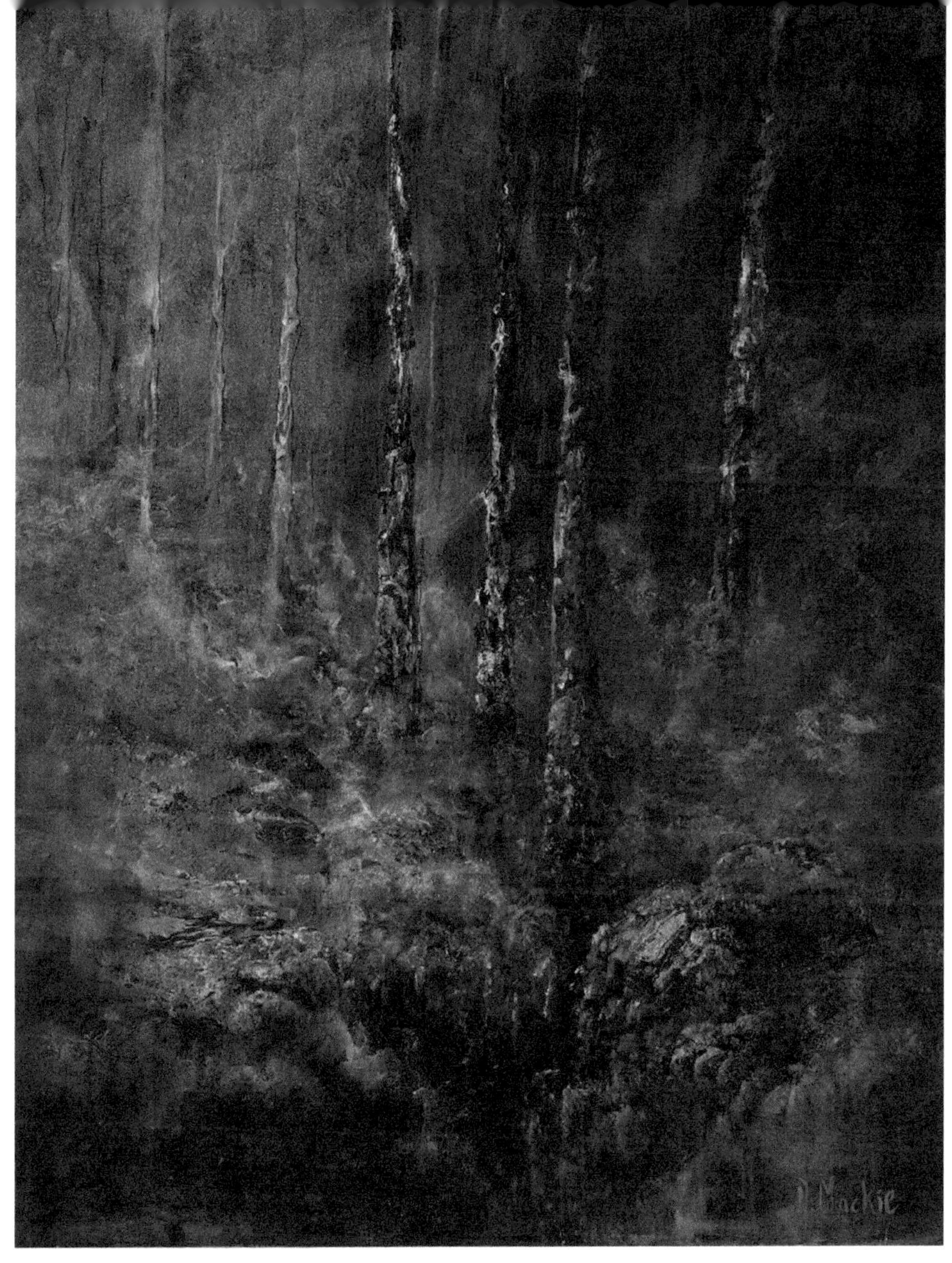

Woodland

Woodland and moss: an interpretation.

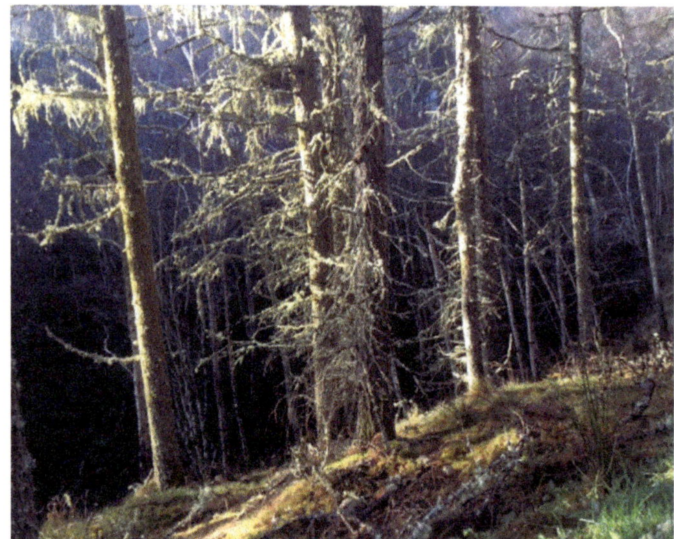

Winter larch

here, and there are different sounds: at the higher levels you hear the wind through the trees; now we have a babbling stream, the crack of branches broken underfoot and perhaps a startled deer or bird. Walking through woodland, with the soaking, decaying leaves rendering down to support the ongoing growth above, I feel a great sense of nature recycling herself.

The experience of walking in woodland in daylight and in the dark is strikingly different. On a bright autumn day, I enjoy the smells of the damp leaves and how the woodland floor is dappled by sunlight. But when darkness falls, other senses are aroused. You listen harder because you cannot see so much. The sound of a breaking twig, the hoot of an owl or the scream of a vixen can send you into a state of trepidation.

Silver Birch at the Waterside

Gentle movement in the water disturbs the reflected trunks.

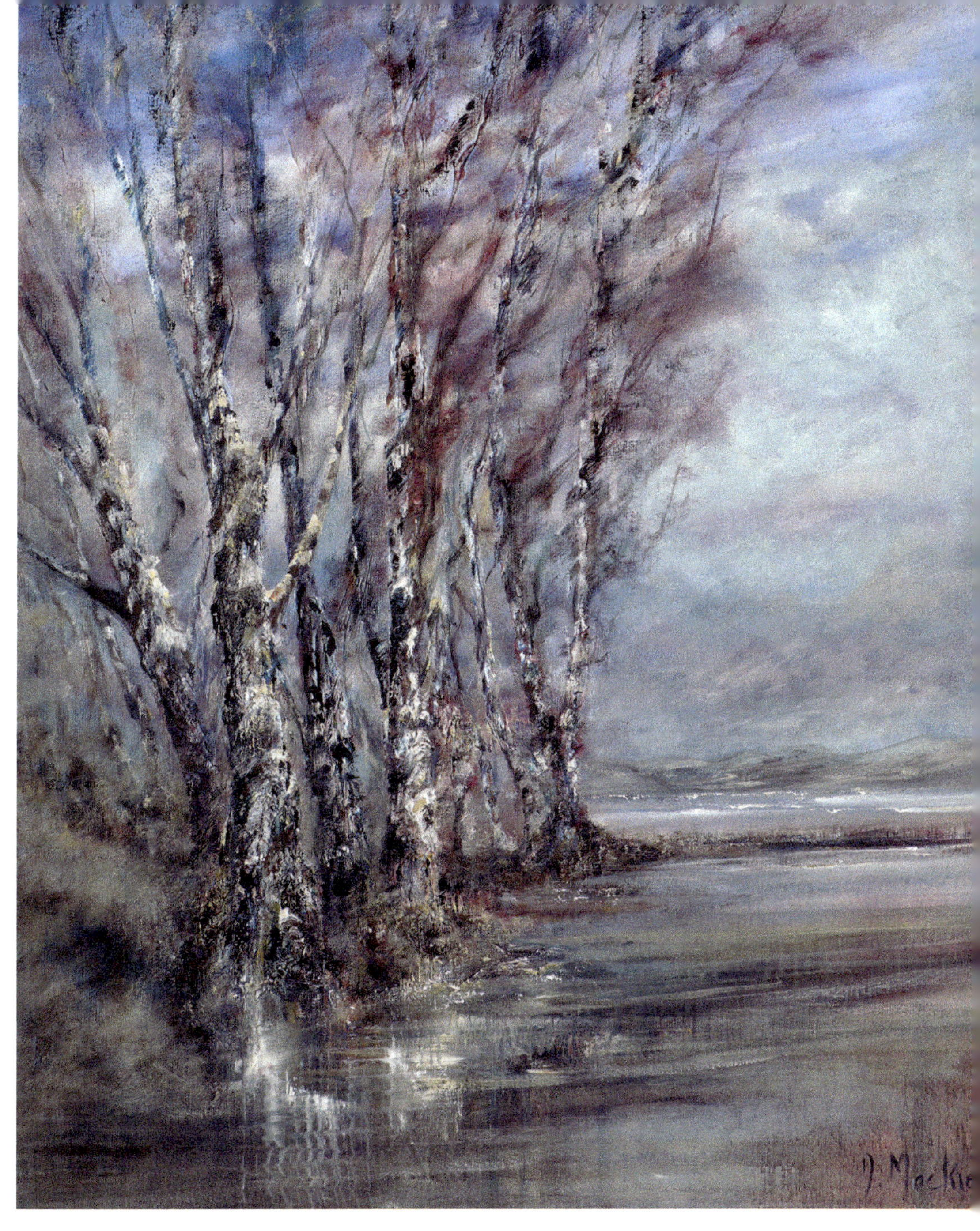

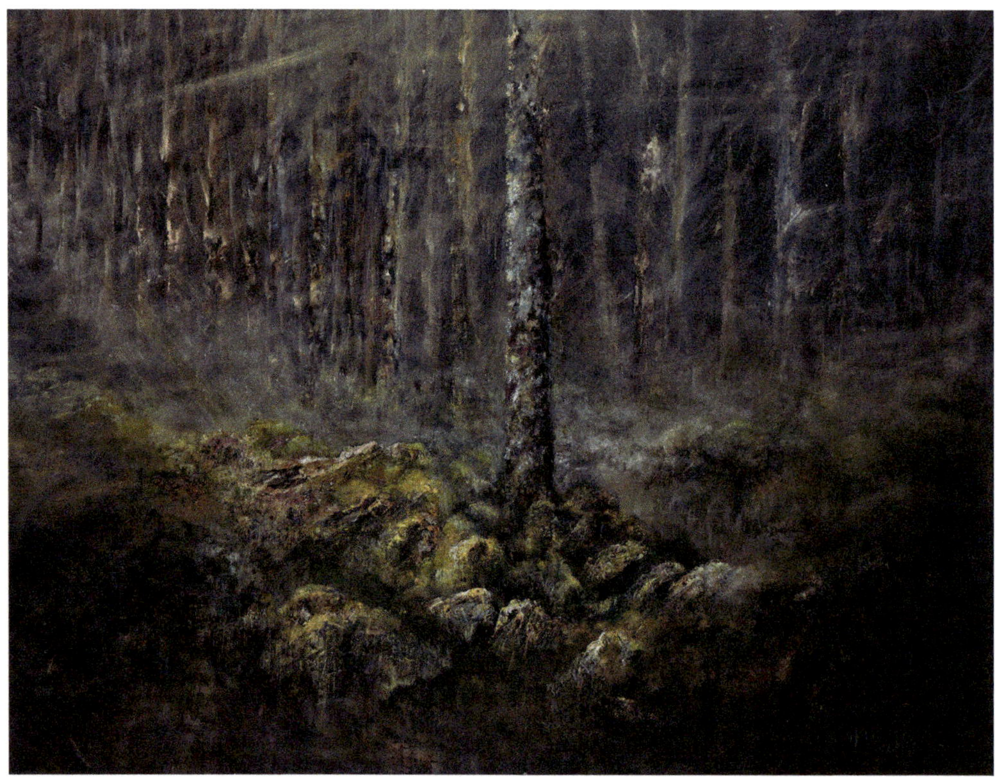

Mossed Boulders (above)

Large moss-cushioned boulders flourish in the damp woods, a variety of
greens against grey hues in the low light.

Birch Trees in Autumn (right)

This study observes how the silver birches actually come out of the ground.
I chose to focus on the textures and colours of the bark.

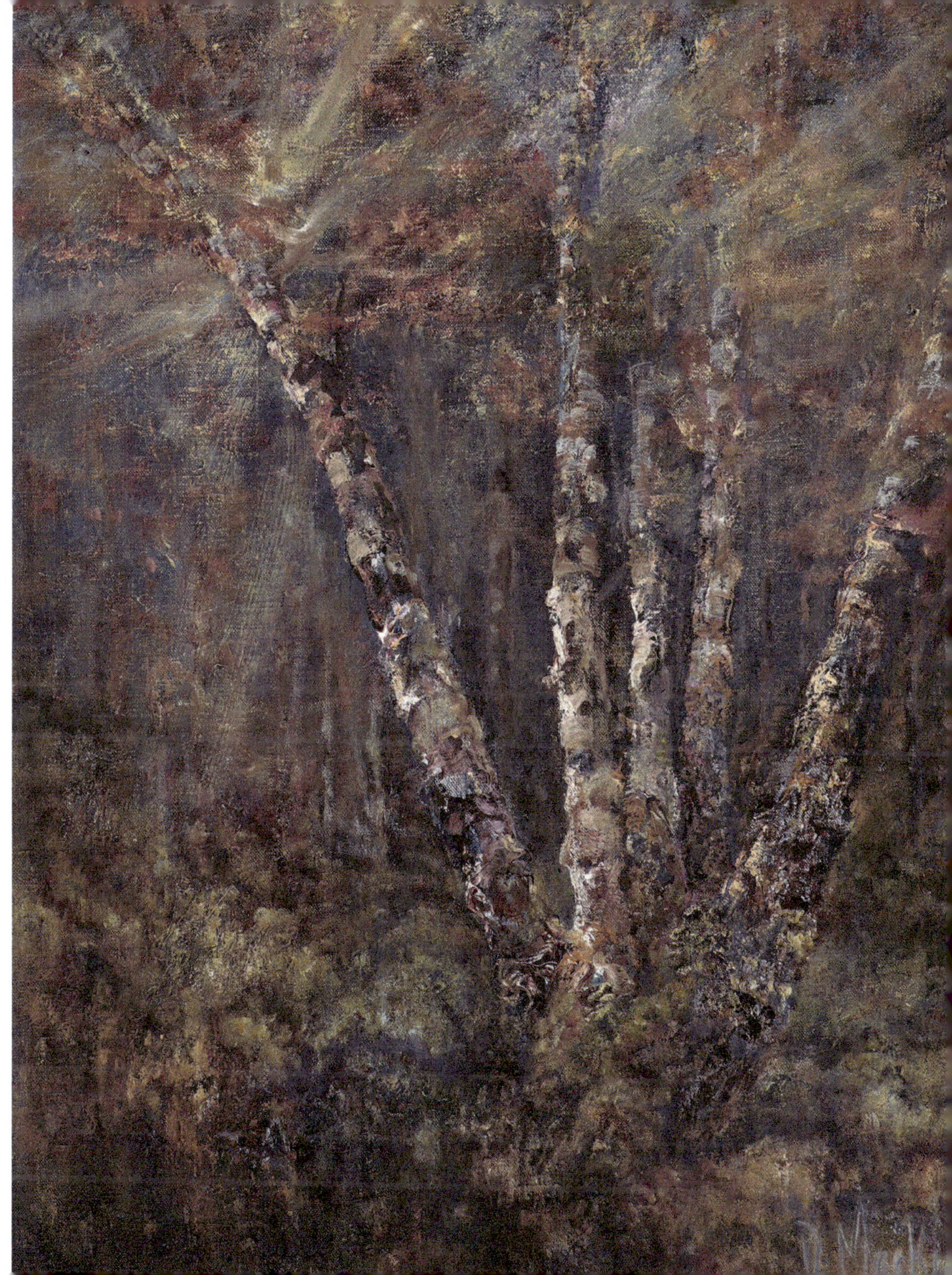

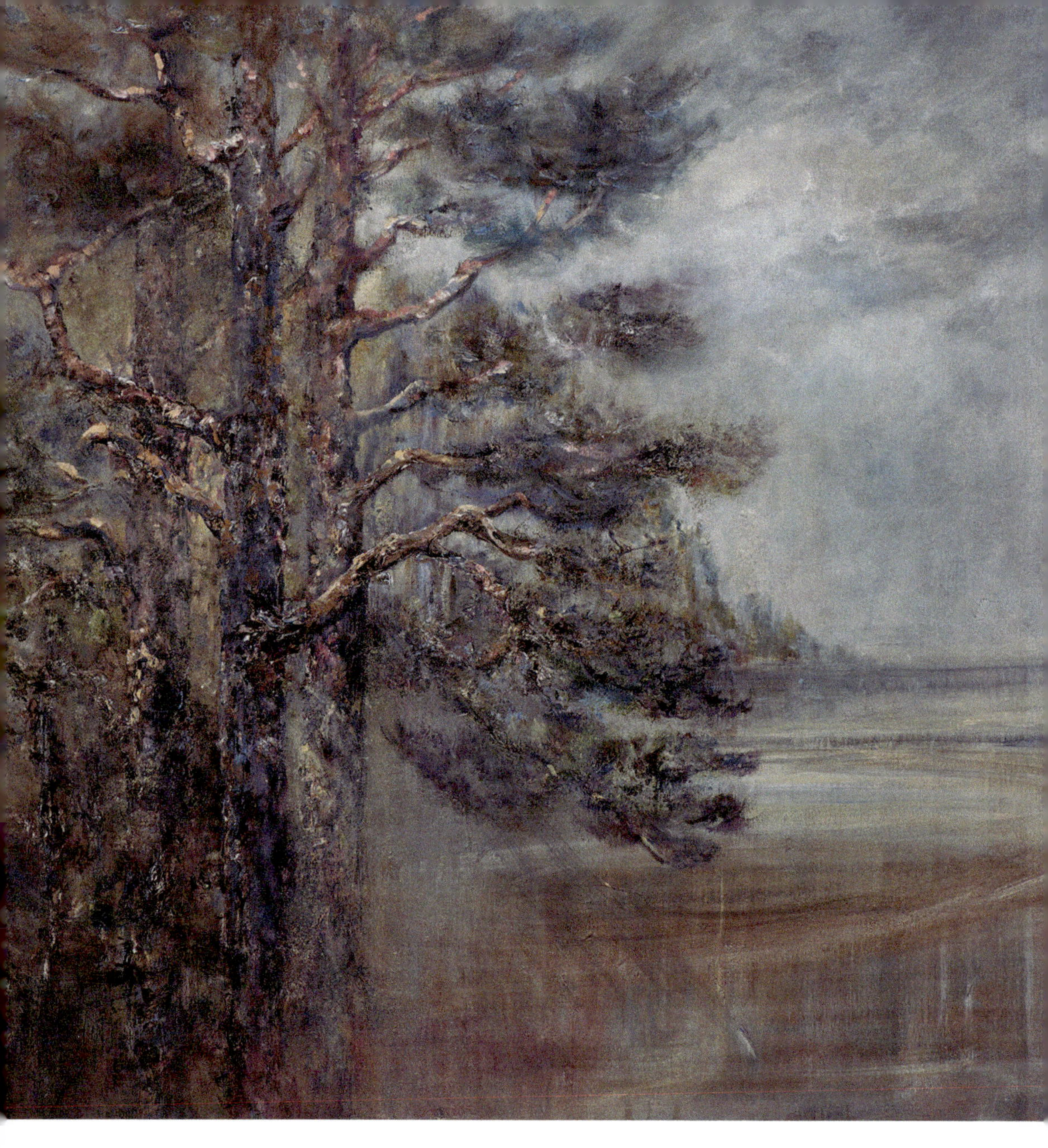

Scots Pine

Caledonian pinewood, sturdy branches tinged with pink in morning light.

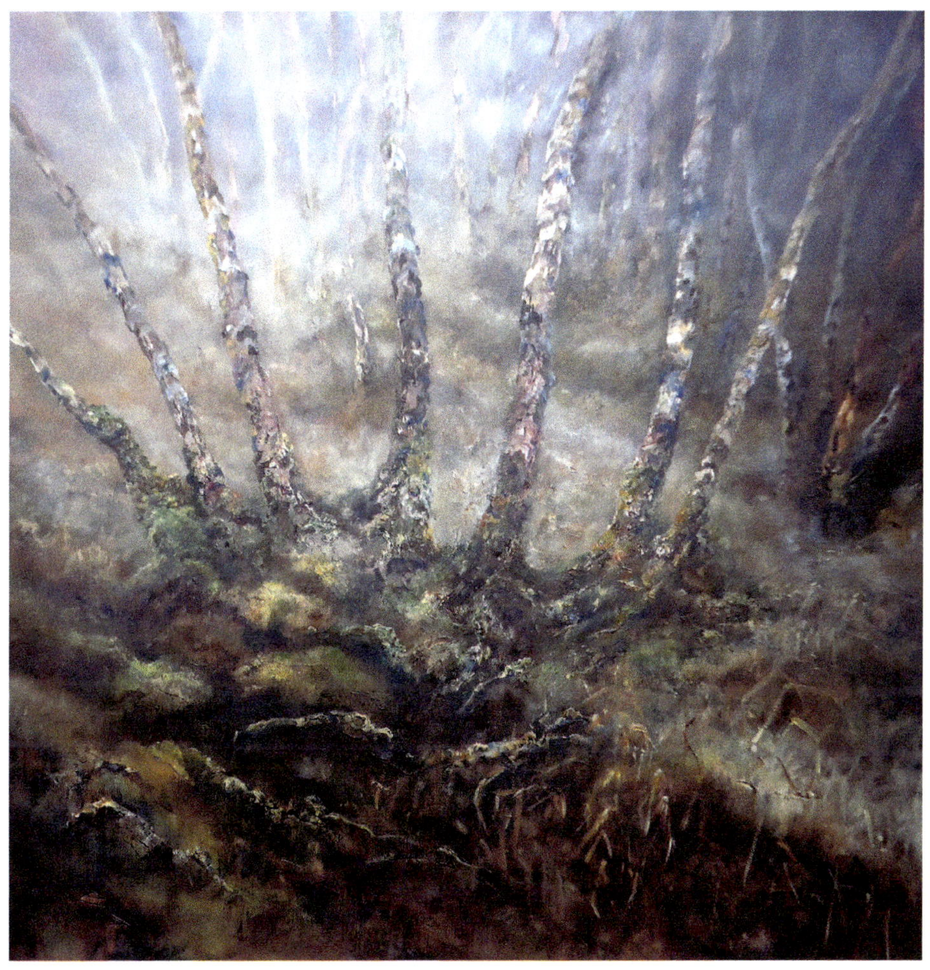

Early Morning Silver Birch

The ghostly forms of silver birch trees in the twilight. Terracotta bracken
fronds and mosses, showing an acidic lime green, add to the palette.

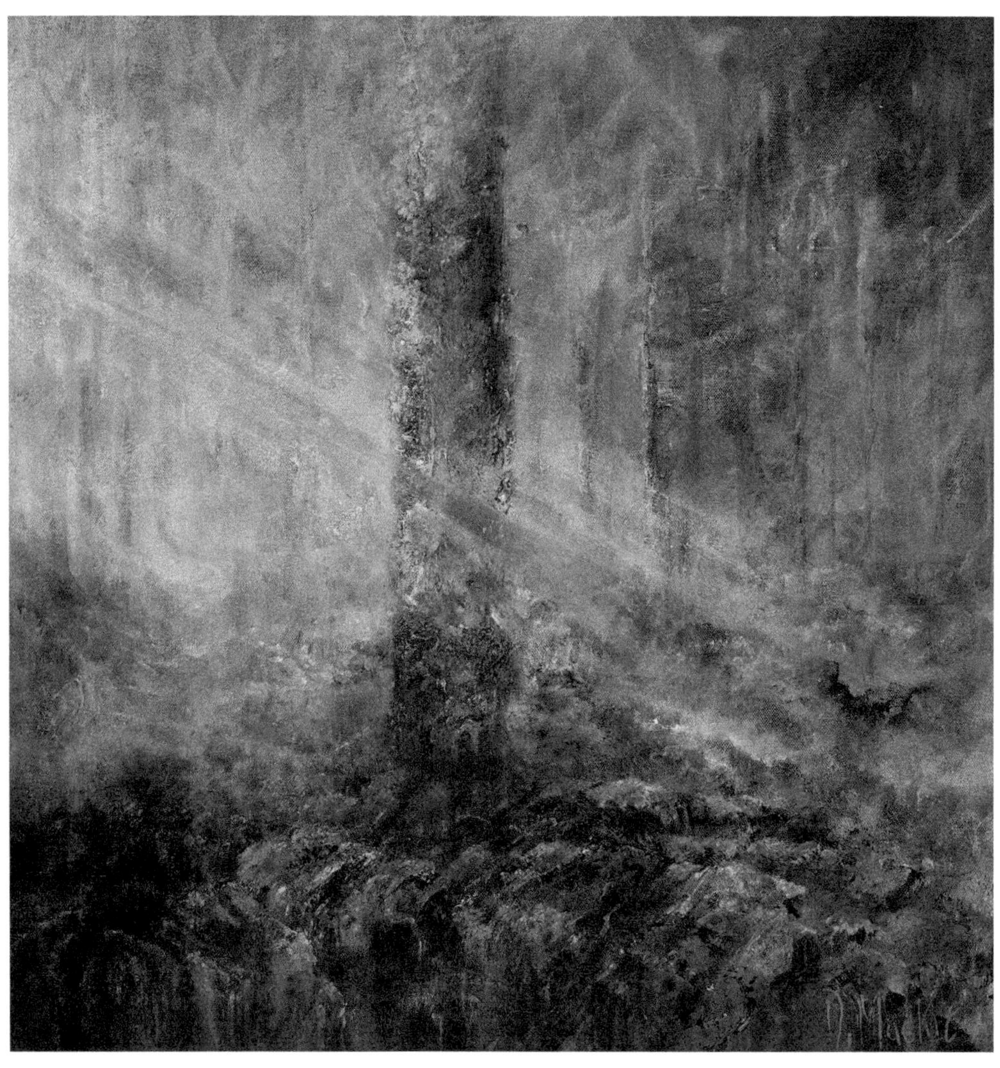

Winter Sunshine

Shafts of light penetrating the forest.

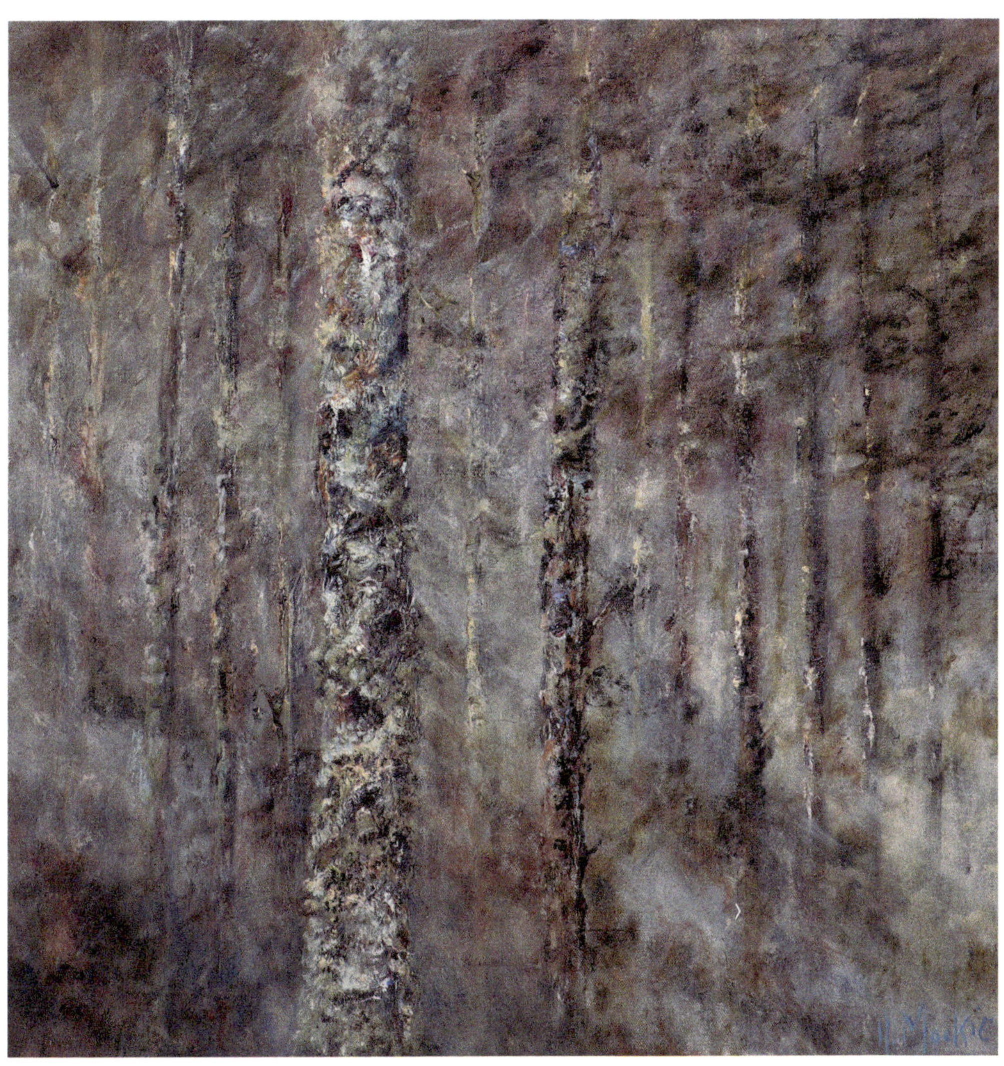

Winter Trees

Lichen dresses straight pine trunks with shades of textured grey and sage.

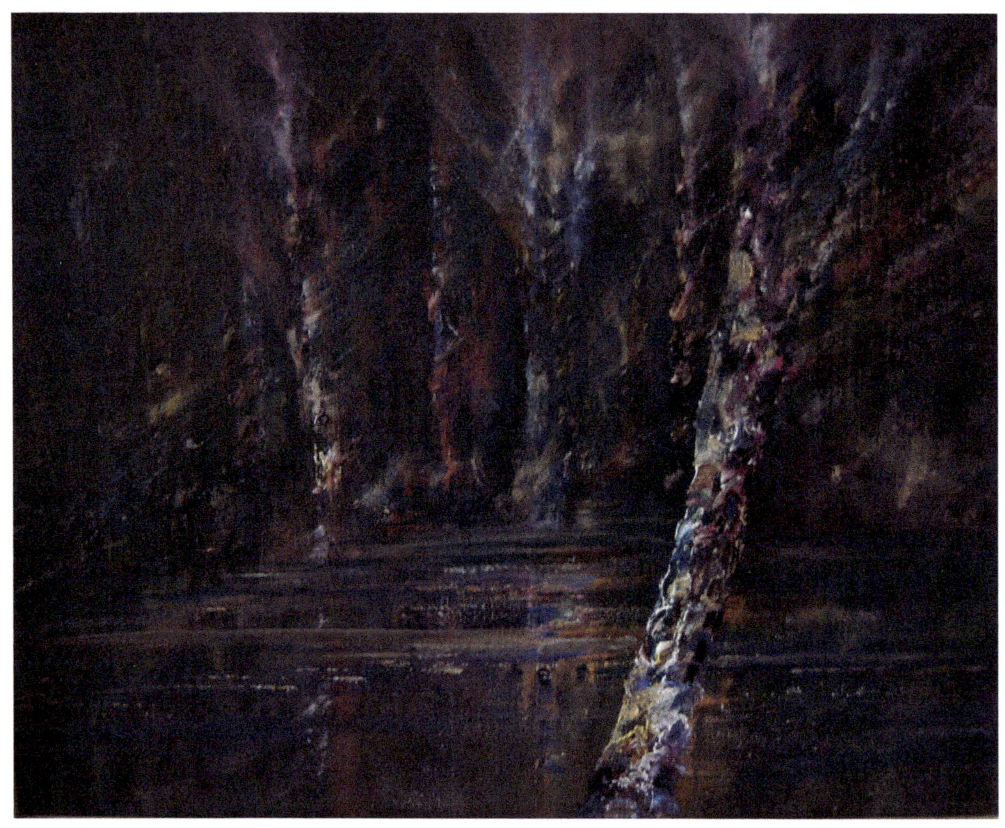

Wet Woodland

A flooded area of Dunvegan Wood in half light – difficult to distinguish
between the trees and their reflections.

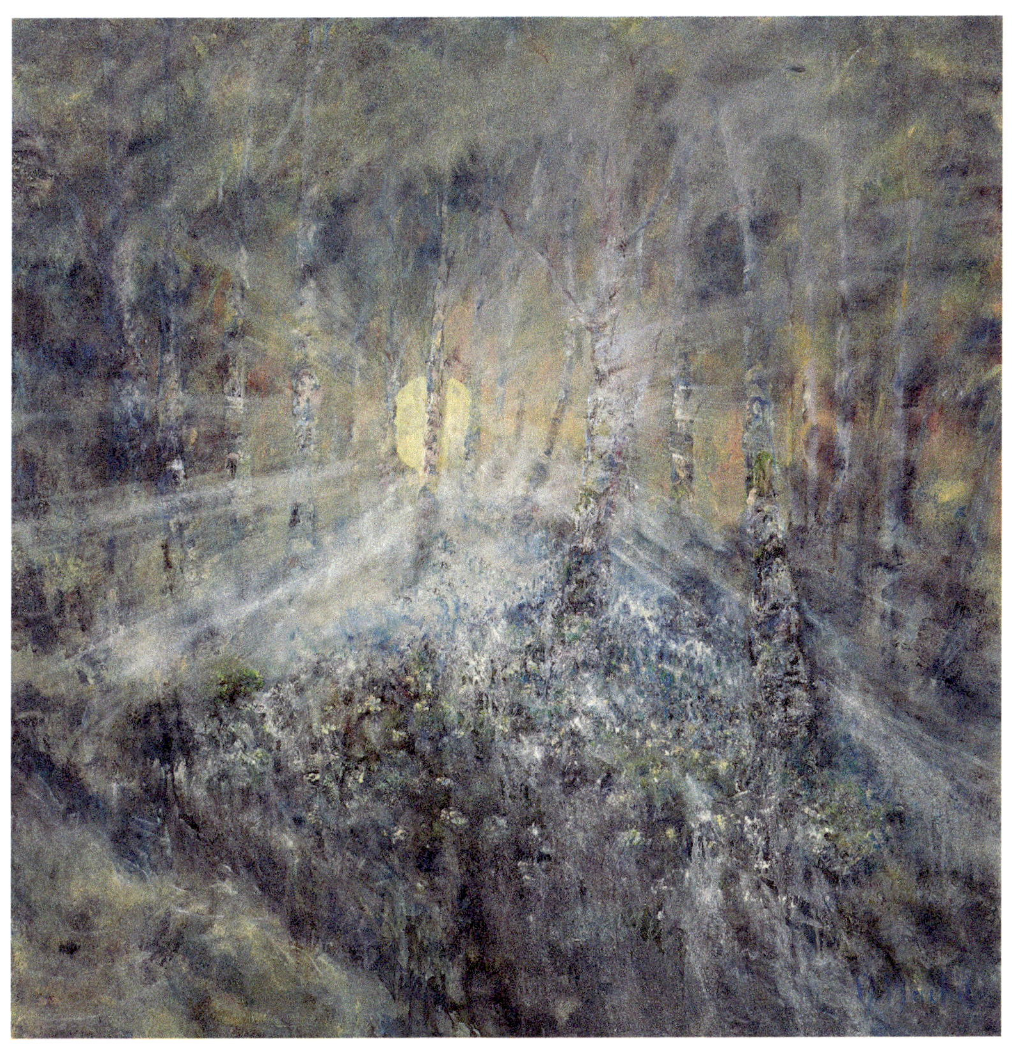

Spring

Sunrise, light flowing across a haze of bluebells and primroses.

Cloud Falls

Rocks, bursing through swathes of cloud.

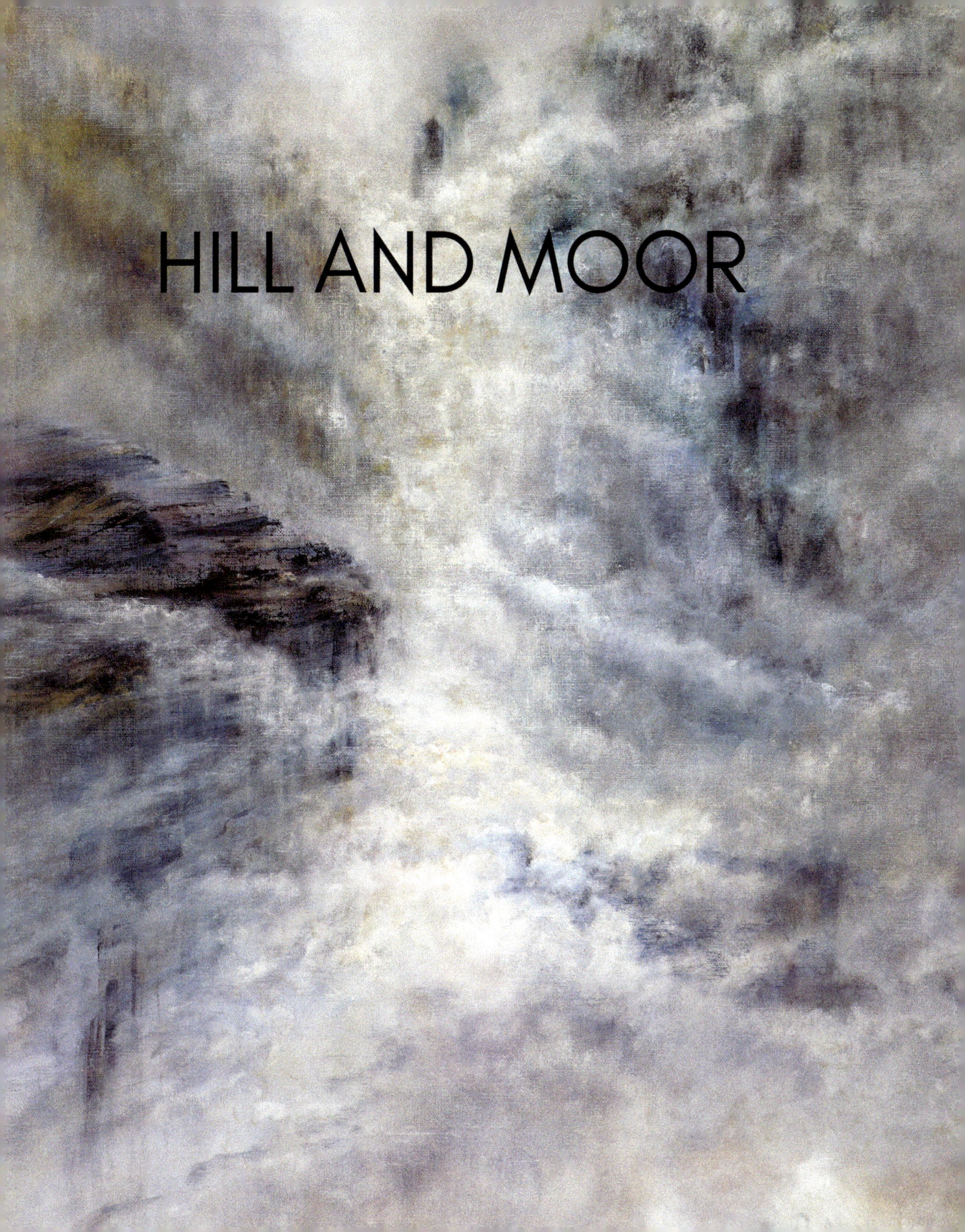

HILL AND MOOR

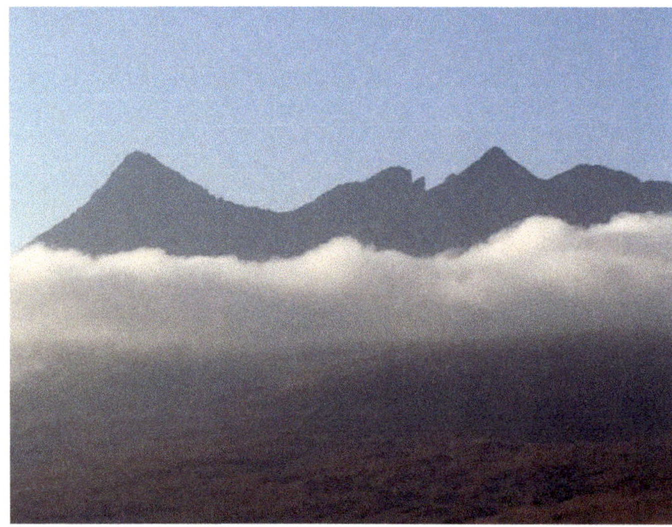

The Black Cuillin

THE BLACK CUILLIN and the Red Cuillin ranges, both rising to over 3,000ft at their highest points, are a magnet for climbers from all over the world. Glen Sligachan, which runs between the ranges, is one of my favourite places. In autumn and winter, the hills that lead up to the mountains are at their most dramatic, especially when bathed in low sunlight, the bronzes of the died-back bracken contrasting with the inky black of the hills. The whole sense of the area is both magnificent and threatening. The different gradients of the hills beneath the scudding clouds offer strong contrasts of colour; in winter, a palette of indigo, Vandyke brown, light red, Alizarin crimson, Naples yellow and cobalt blue.

This is MacLeod territory. Following an incident in 1577, when 300 MacDonalds were trapped in a large cave on the shoreline of the island of Eigg and were suffocated by the smoke from fires lit at the entrance by the MacLeods. The MacDonalds swore revenge. The following year they landed at Ardmore on Skye and tracked down their enemies to Trumpan, where the MacLeods were attending a service at Kilconan Church. They set fire to the church, burning to death all those within, apart from one young girl who escaped through a window.

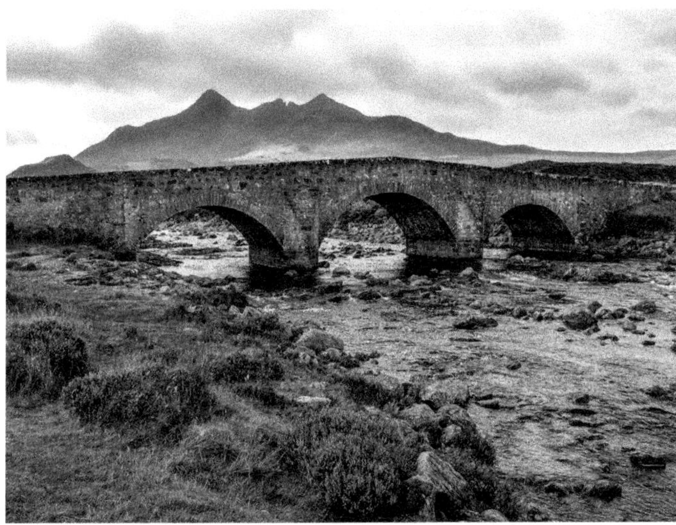

The Old Bridge at Sligachan
(Shutterstock)

The MacLeods, seeing the smoke, chased the MacDonalds down to the shore where their boats were waiting for them. Unfortunately for them, the tide was out and they could not make good their escape. They were at the mercy of the MacLeods, who left none alive. A drystane dyke was toppled over the bodies – hence the name the Battle of the Spoiling of the Dyke.

Living at Borreraig, we discovered we have a close connection to the MacCrimmons, the pipers to the MacLeods, when we read the following in Robert Bruce Campbell's *The MacCrimmon Pipers of Skye: A Tradition Under Siege:*

From a sodden hilltop in a remote corner of one of the most remote areas in western Europe the MacCrimmon pipers brought the world their enduring legacy, piobaireachd.

It seems rather strange to hear this description of where we live! The MacCrimmons founded a piping school at Borreraig in the early 1500s. It is a short walk up this 'sodden hilltop' from our house. The views across Dunvegan Loch and out to the Hebrides on a clear day are breathtaking and there is always the chance of sighting gannets diving and the odd minke whale.

Sheep roam the fields, roads and

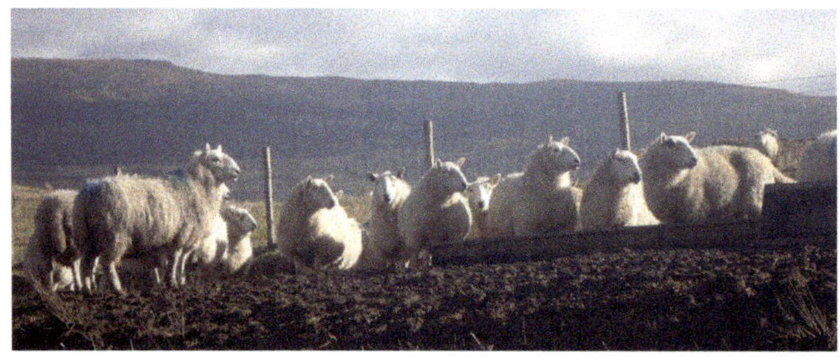

Sheep

communal grazing areas on the hills of Skye. My crofter neighbour often comments that all they want to do is to find different ways of killing themselves. On car journeys or walks, we often have to stop to wrestle with a sheep that has got its head stuck in a gate or fence, or has cast herself – which means that having laid down, in struggling to get up she falls onto her back and is then stuck. Until the sheep is righted, it will be at the mercy of the crows and gulls. To see a dead one, despatched or left to die, without its eyes or tongue, following a visit from crows and gulls, is not uncommon.

Sheep present quite a challenge to visitors to Skye, but there is no point in being impatient when you have a flock in front of you. They will find their way onto the verges in their own time. The biggest danger is when a ewe is grazing in a ditch completely out of sight on one side of the road and its lamb is in a ditch on the other; suddenly the lamb bounces out to join its mum and gives the driver a heart attack.

However diligent a crofter might be, there are always fatalities among lambs and ewes. Spring brings the joy of the skipping lambs (though perhaps less so for the ewes, who get pretty sick of them, as their back ends are practically lifted off the ground by the lambs' ferocious suckling).

Sheep's View (right)
An elderly sheep makes its careful way along a treacherous path.

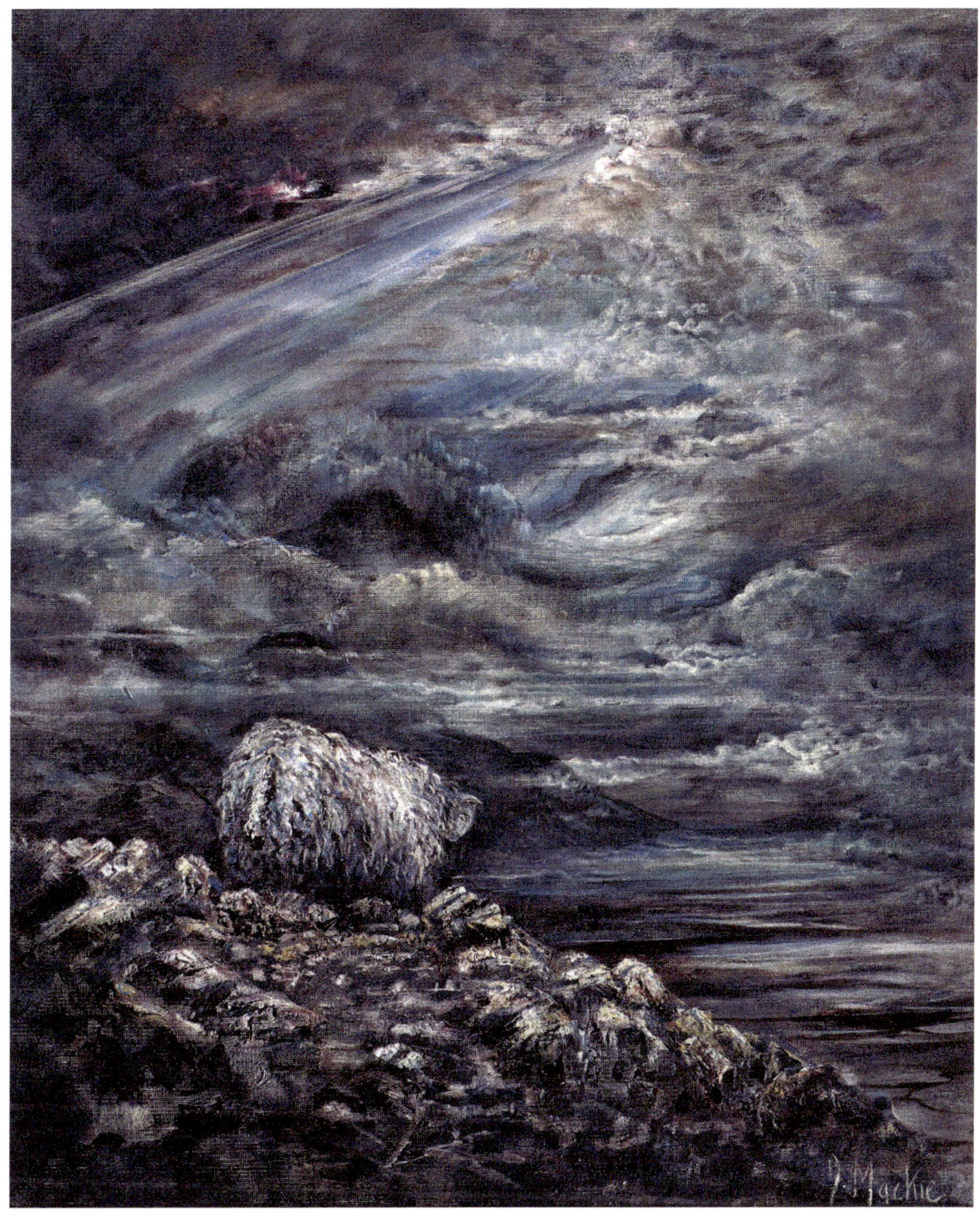

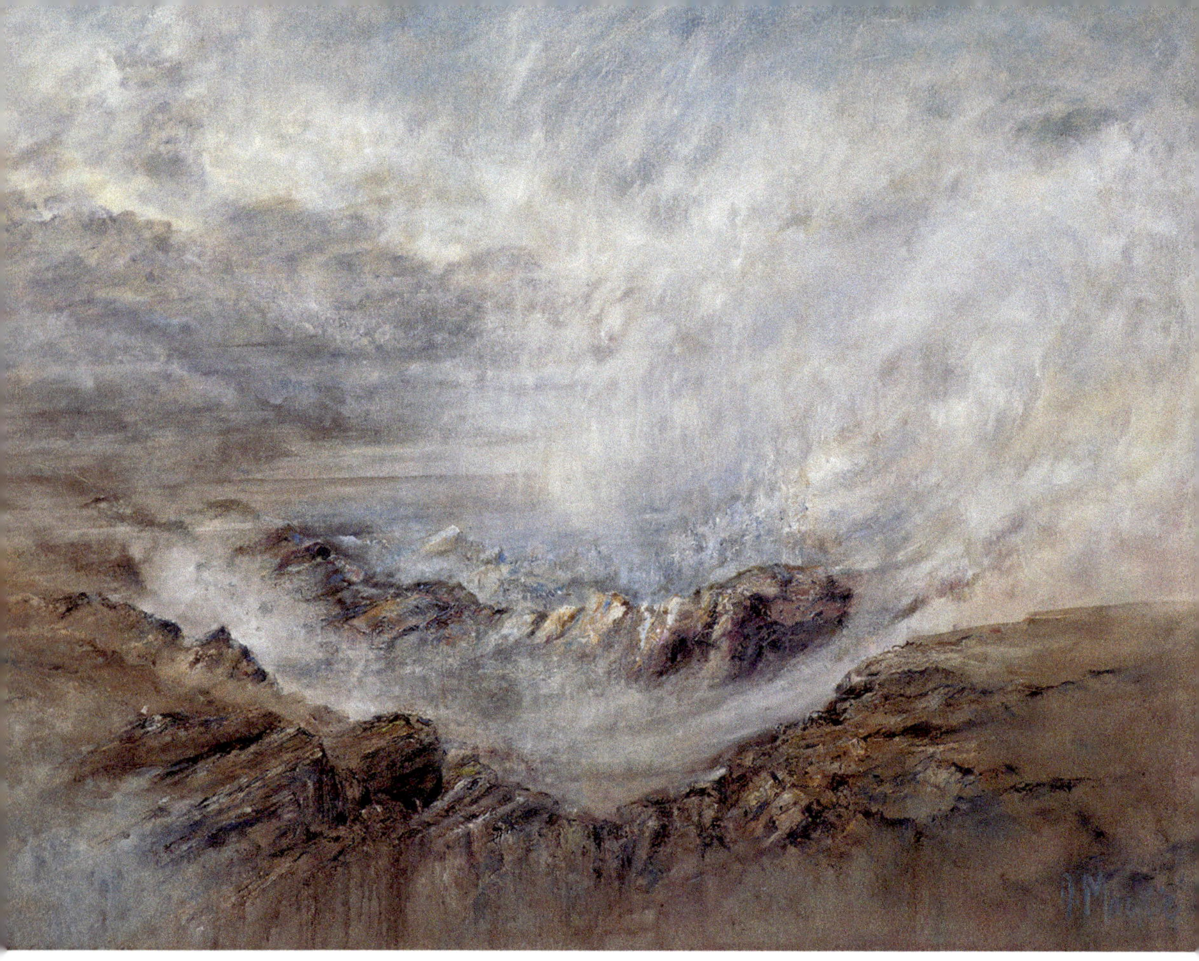

In the Hills (above)

At 4ft x 3ft, one of the largest canvases I have worked on. My objective was
to create a sense of enormous space, with rain showers intermingling with
the mist.

Waterfall (right)

Falling water interrupted by rocks.

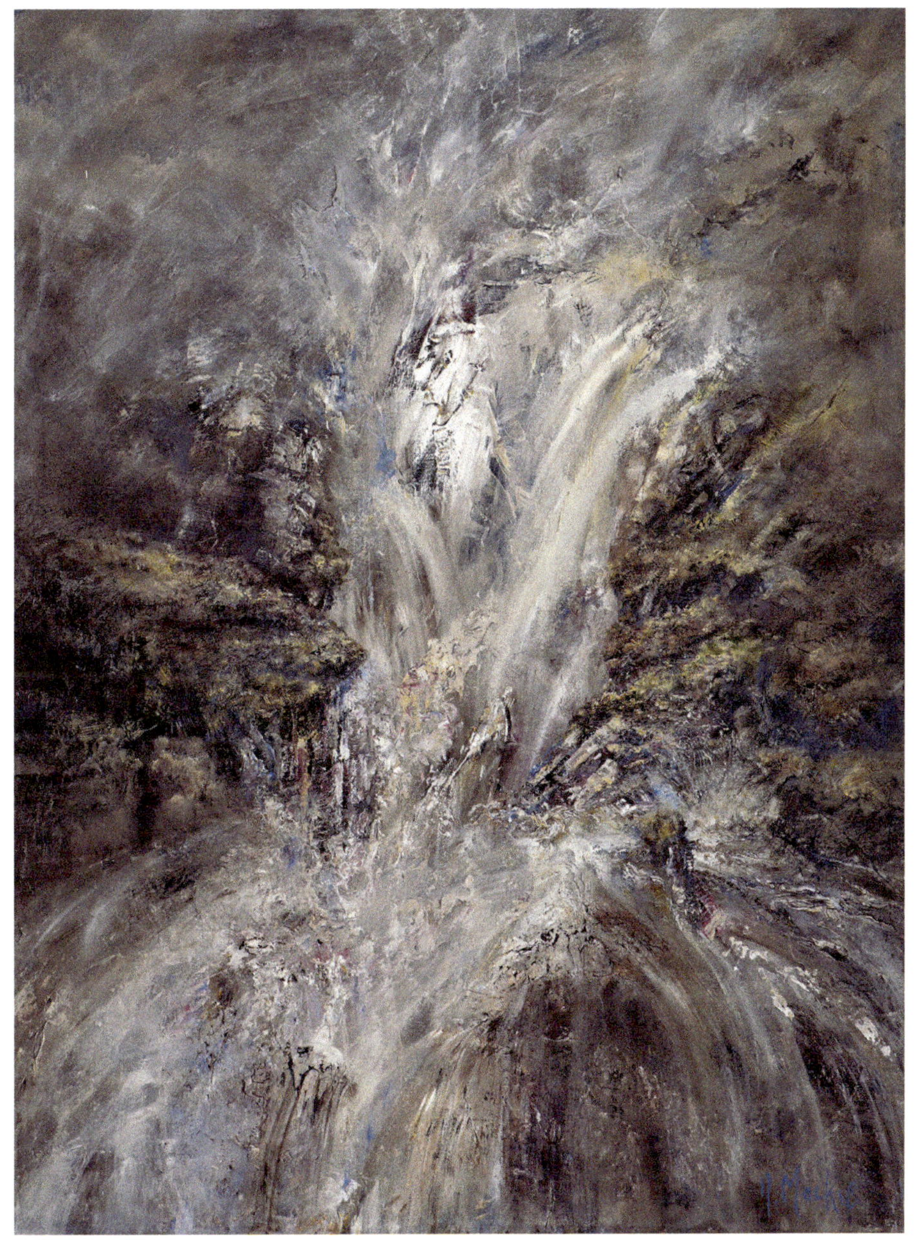

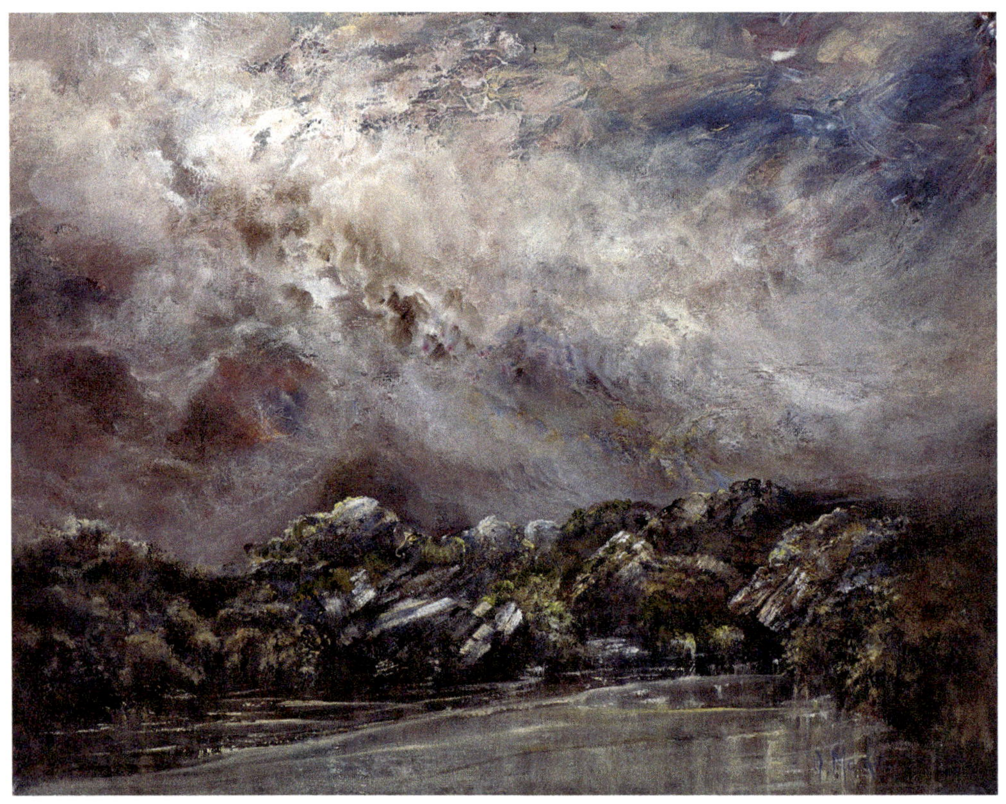

Highland Pool

Threatening clouds overhead, distant mountains, the last of the sunlight
reflected in the small lochans shining in this rugged terrain..

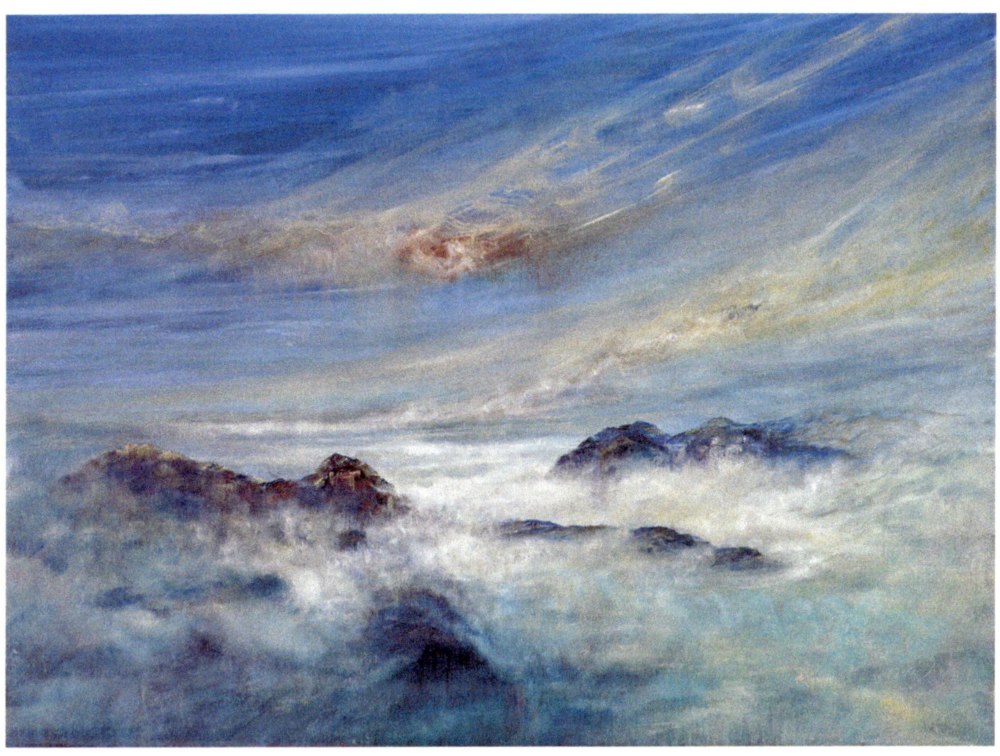

Above Clouds

To be at a level where the mountains are emerging through a cloud bank
gives you a sense of entering another world.

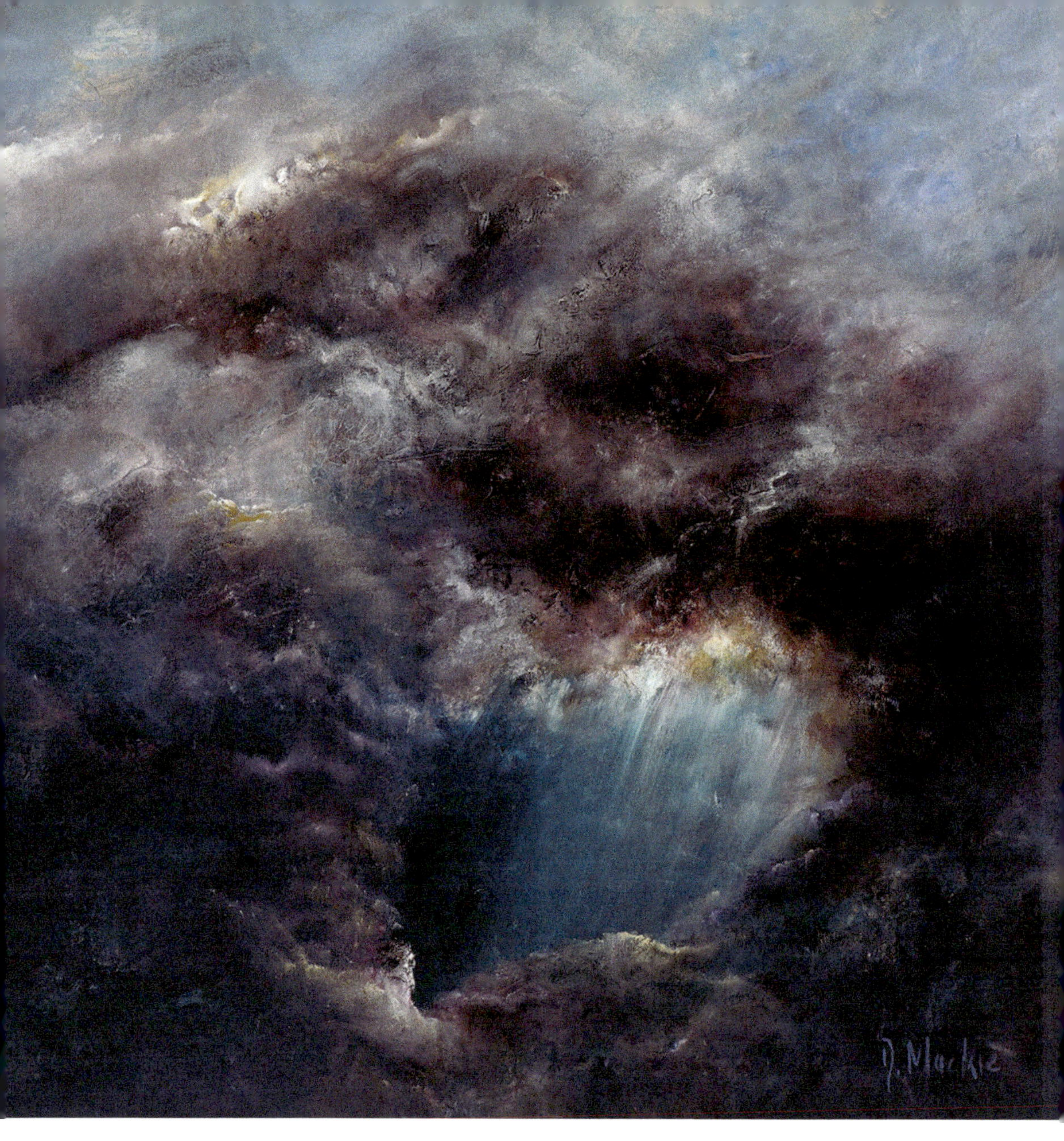

Hole in the Cloud

The expanse of sky revealed through cloud gives a sense of infinity.

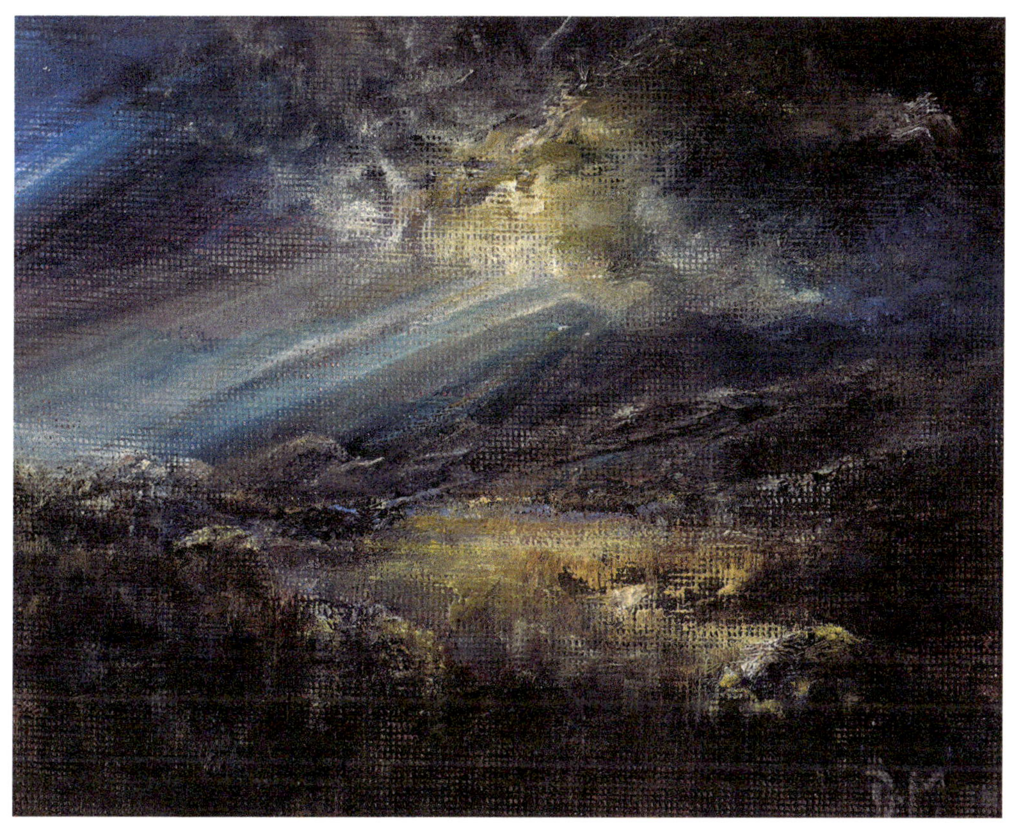

Evening, Glen Sligachan

Storm passing over the moor.

Skye (overleaf)

Capturing the essence of Skye as I experience it, an opera of light and shape.

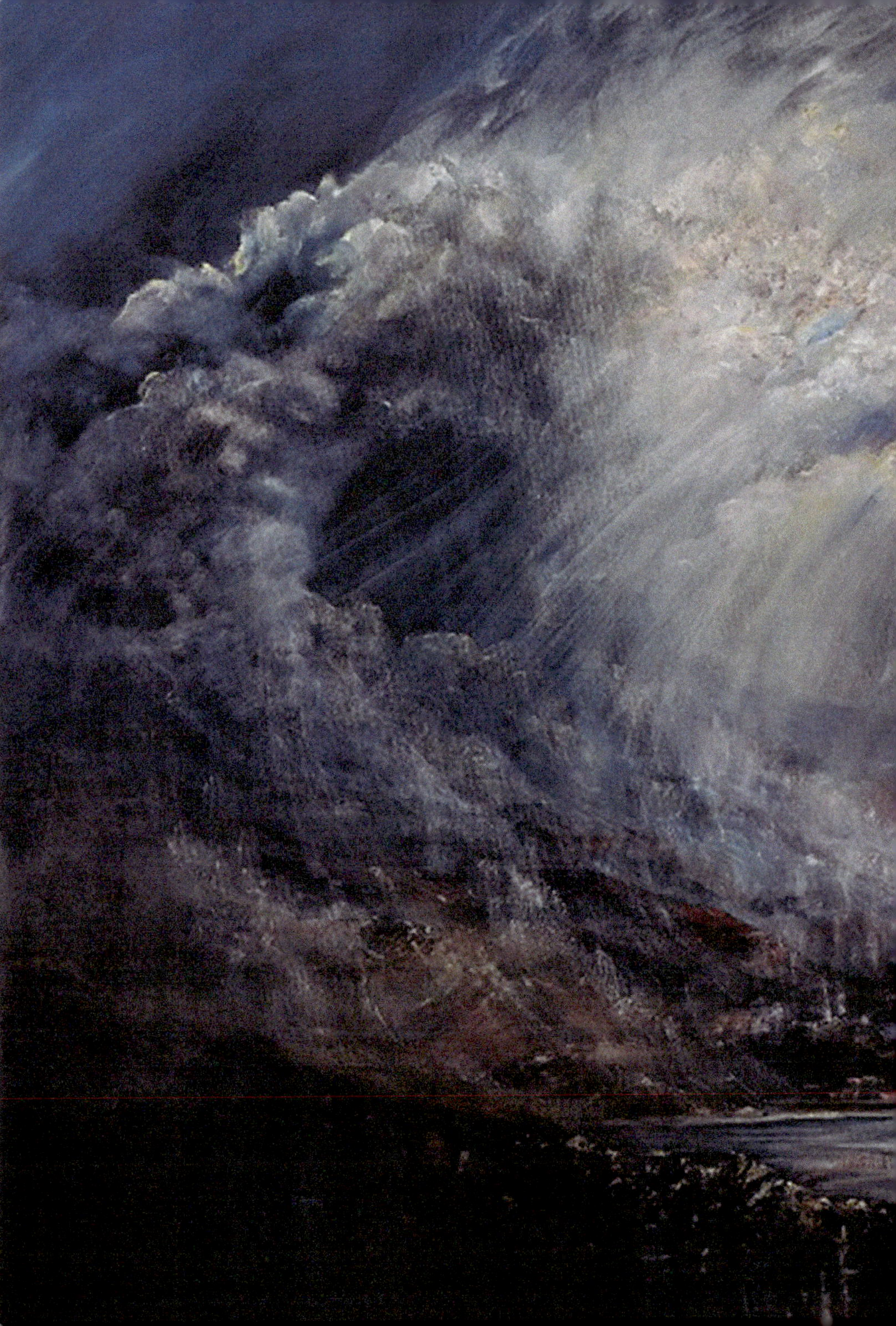

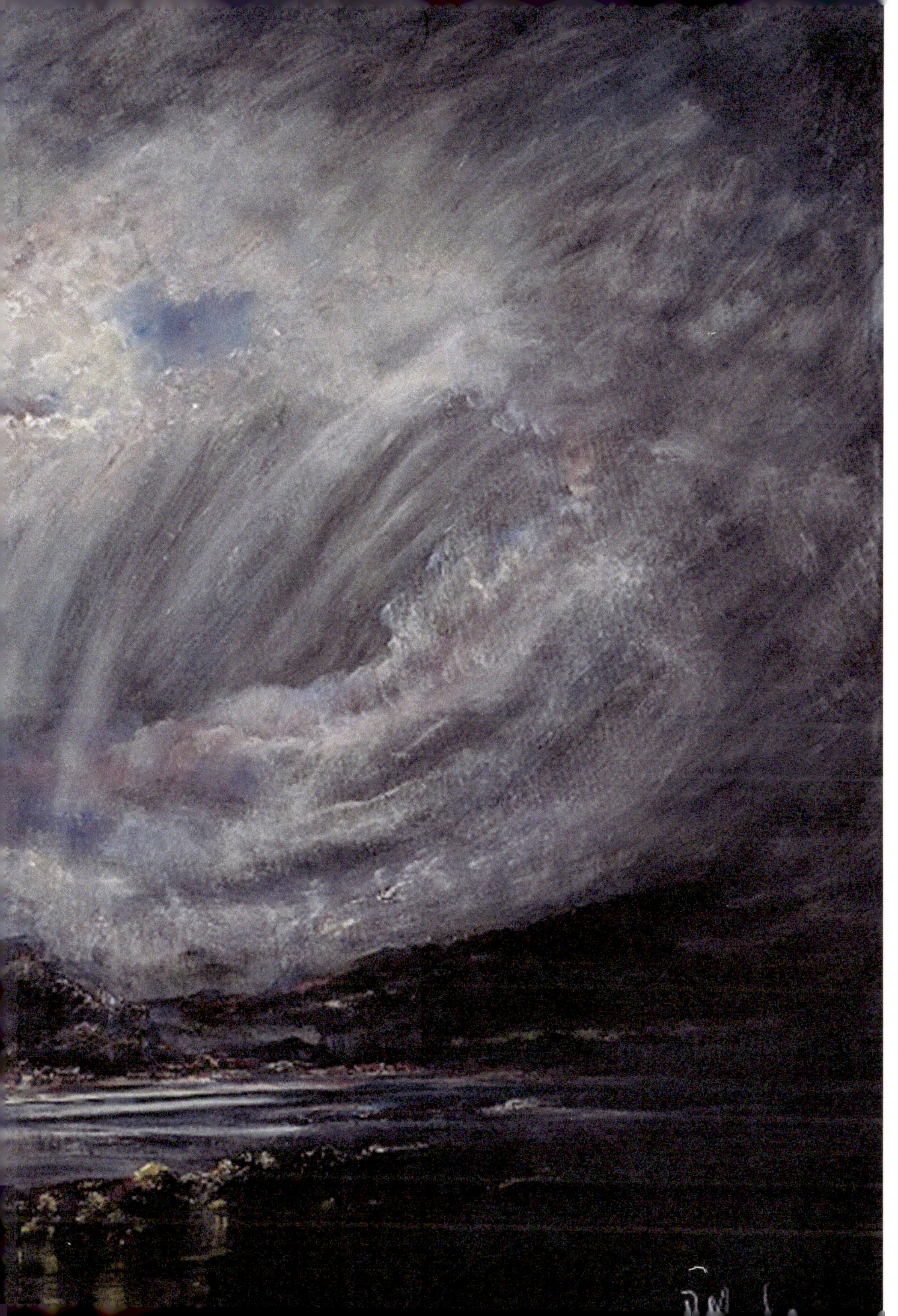

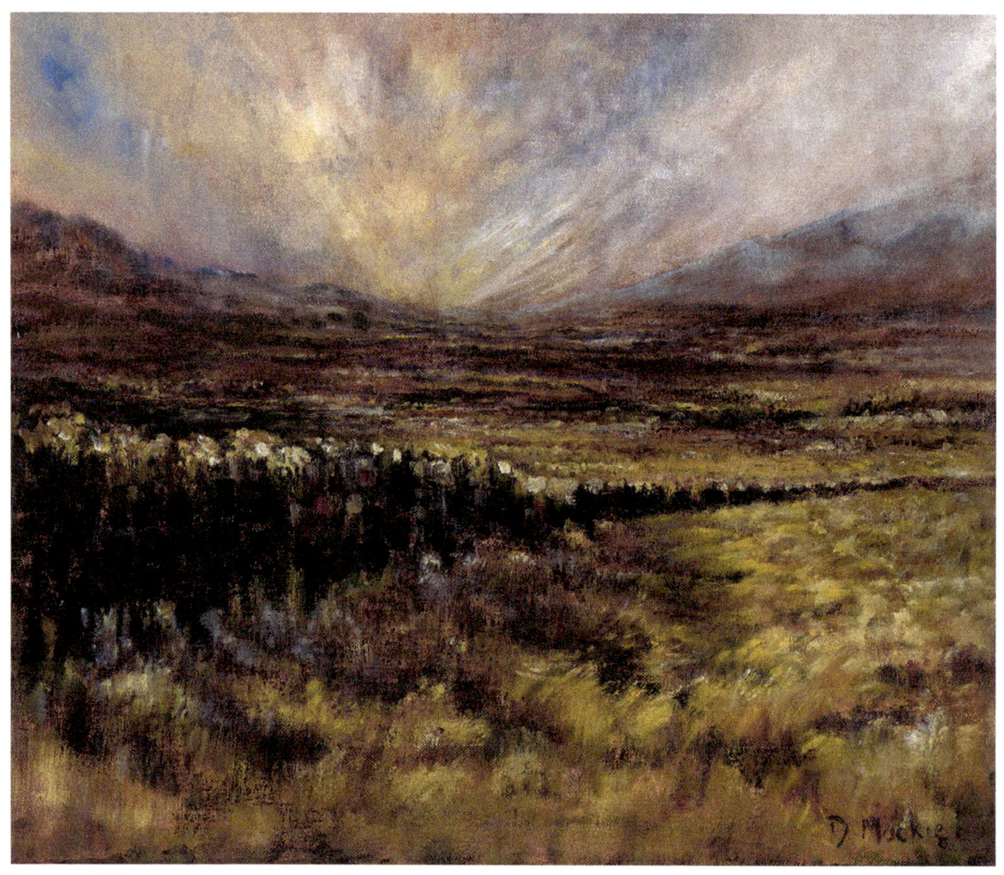

Peatbog

Crofters are still cutting peat each year from this site in Skinidin, but
I am sure that the days of cutting peat for fuel on Skye are numbered.

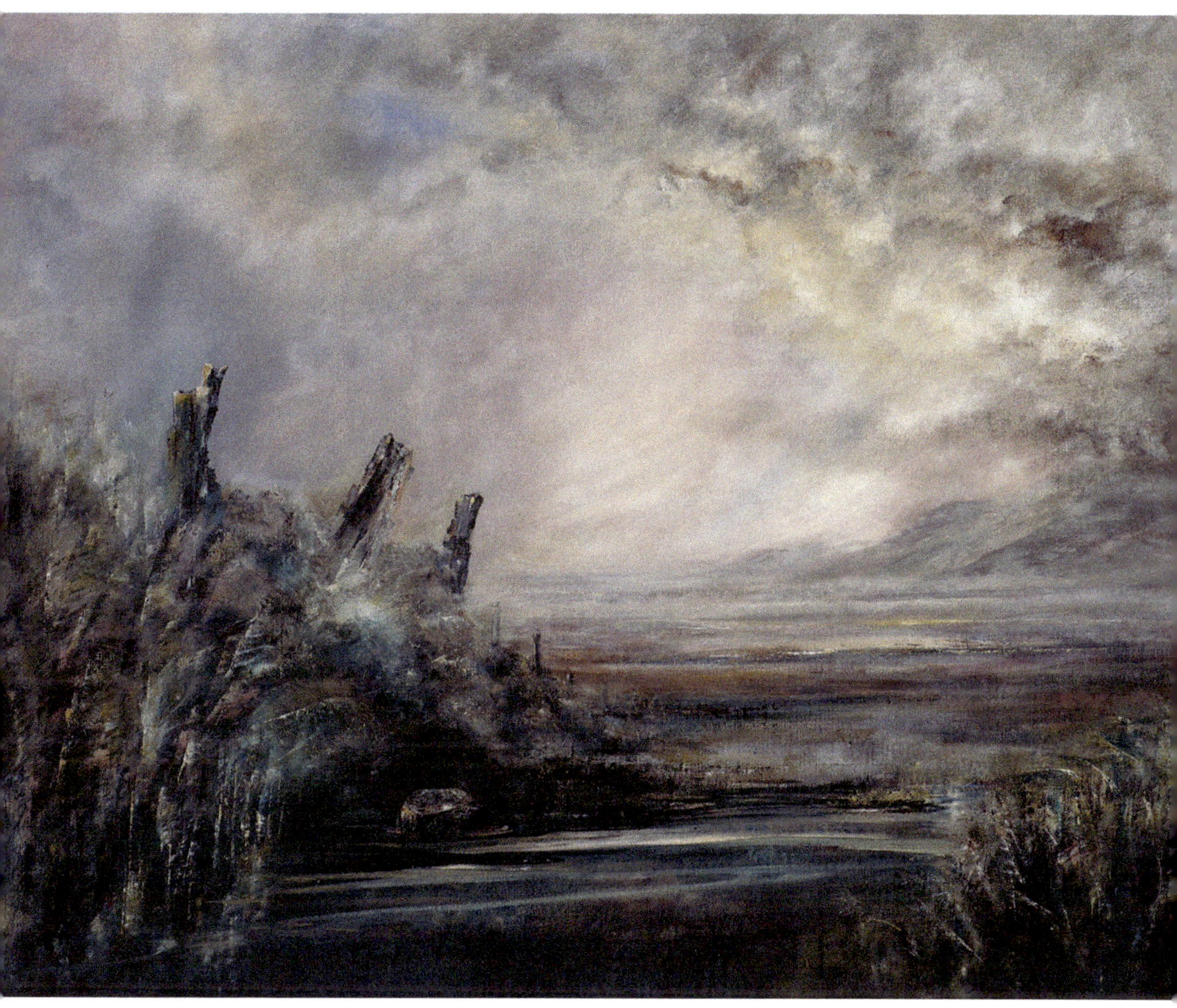

Fence Posts

These fence posts have become host to lichens and insects. Nature has
made her claim and will in time return what is man-made to the ground.

Head of the Waterfall

Full moon above a waterfall.

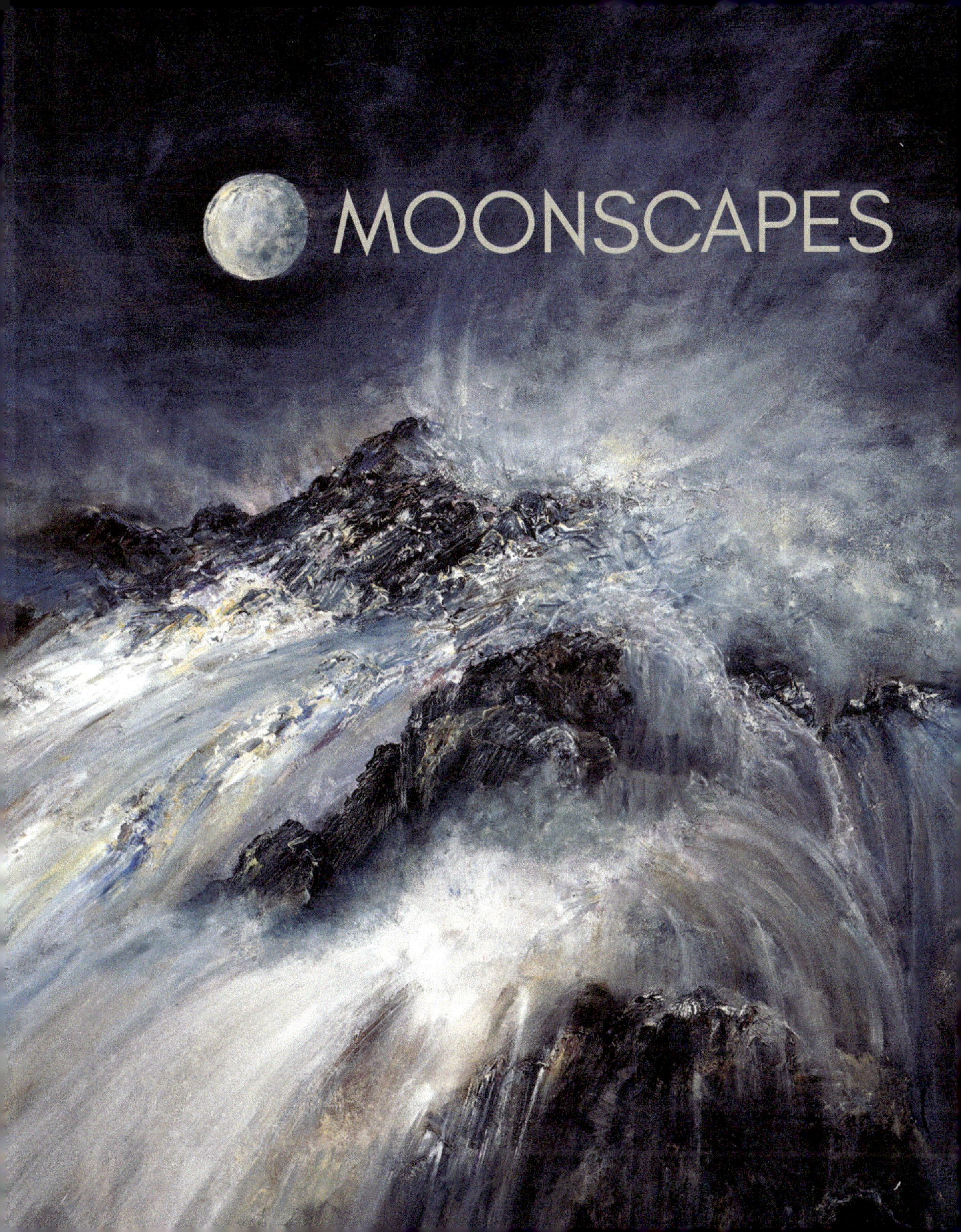

MOONSCAPES

EVERY NIGHT BEFORE I go to bed I seek out the moon. It stimulates in me so many thought processes and emotions. The sheer distance between us is challenging to comprehend; and then, there is the hidden dark side. It makes me ask, what might be going on out there… could there be life beyond the planetary system that we are currently familiar with? The moon has been in orbit around the Earth for millennia before we evolved. I see it as a presence we are accountable to, a silent witness to all our successes and failures.

I sometimes wonder whether the human race has really made such great progress since our conception. In a sense, we are yet to leave the room.

Three years ago, a friend showed me a photograph of the moon which she had taken and it caught my imagination. I embarked on a painterly voyage of discovery. To form a night-time palette, the best results came from a proportional mix of indigo, Vandyke brown and ultramarine. The moon never ceases to be a mesmerising image for me to interpret.

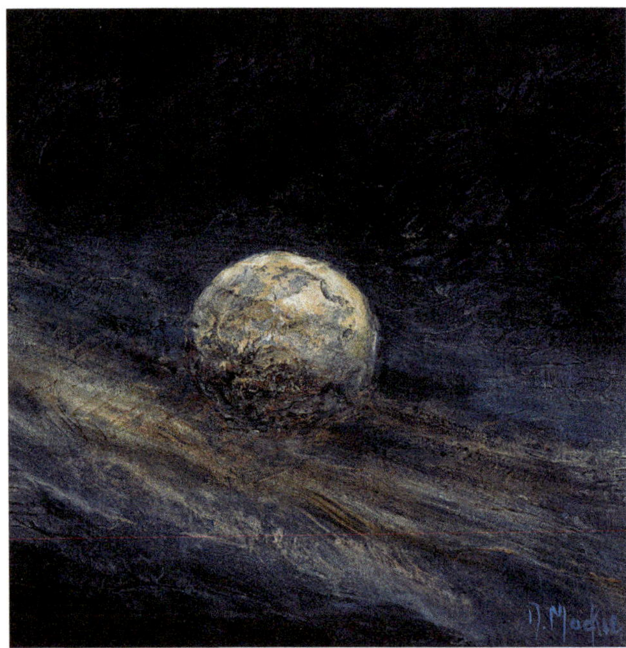

Sarah's Moon

This painting is named for the friend whose photograph began my fascination in painting the moon's landscape and her many moods.

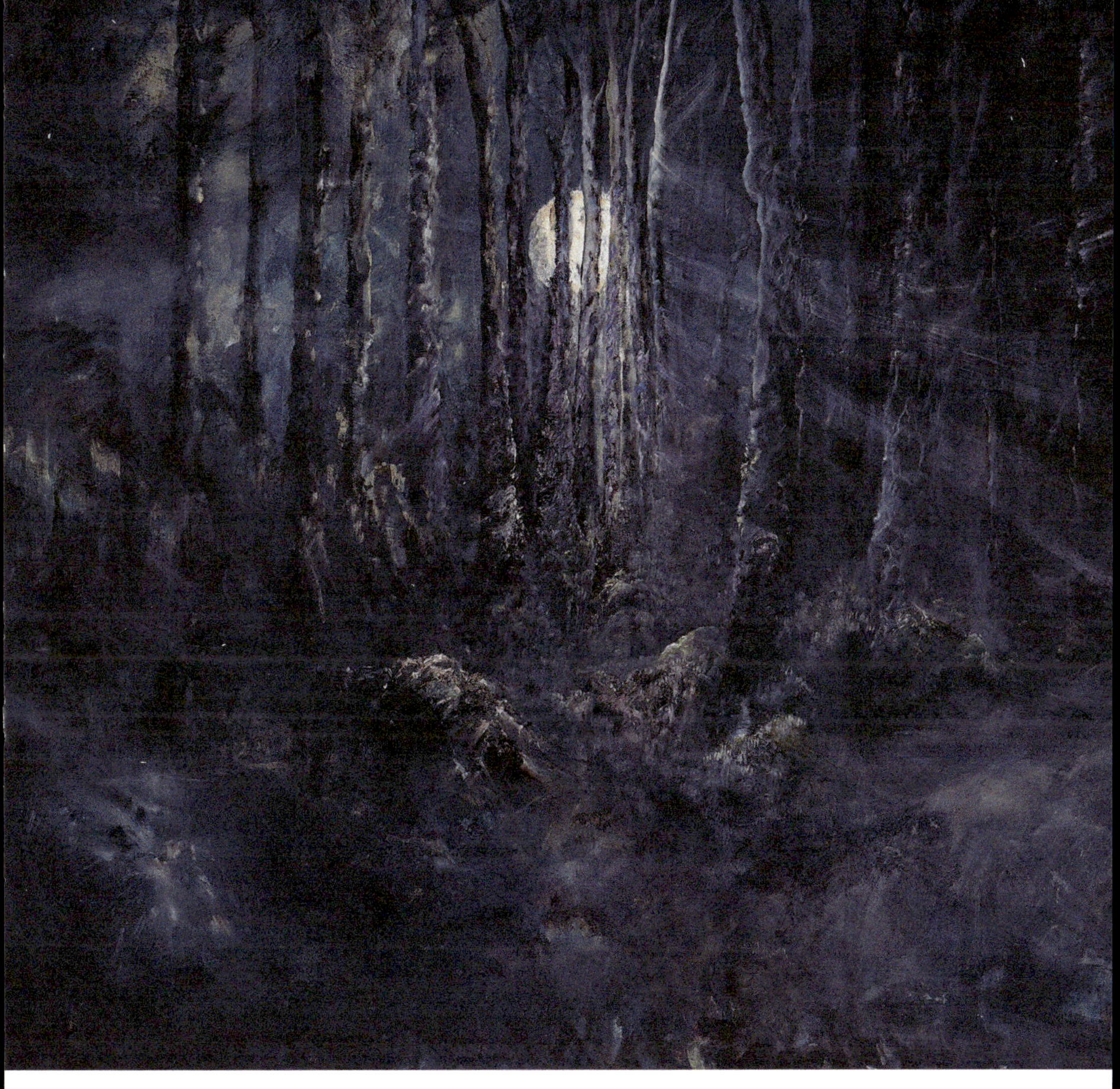

Moon Through Trees

Moonlight reflected on the moist tree trunks and on the woodland floor.

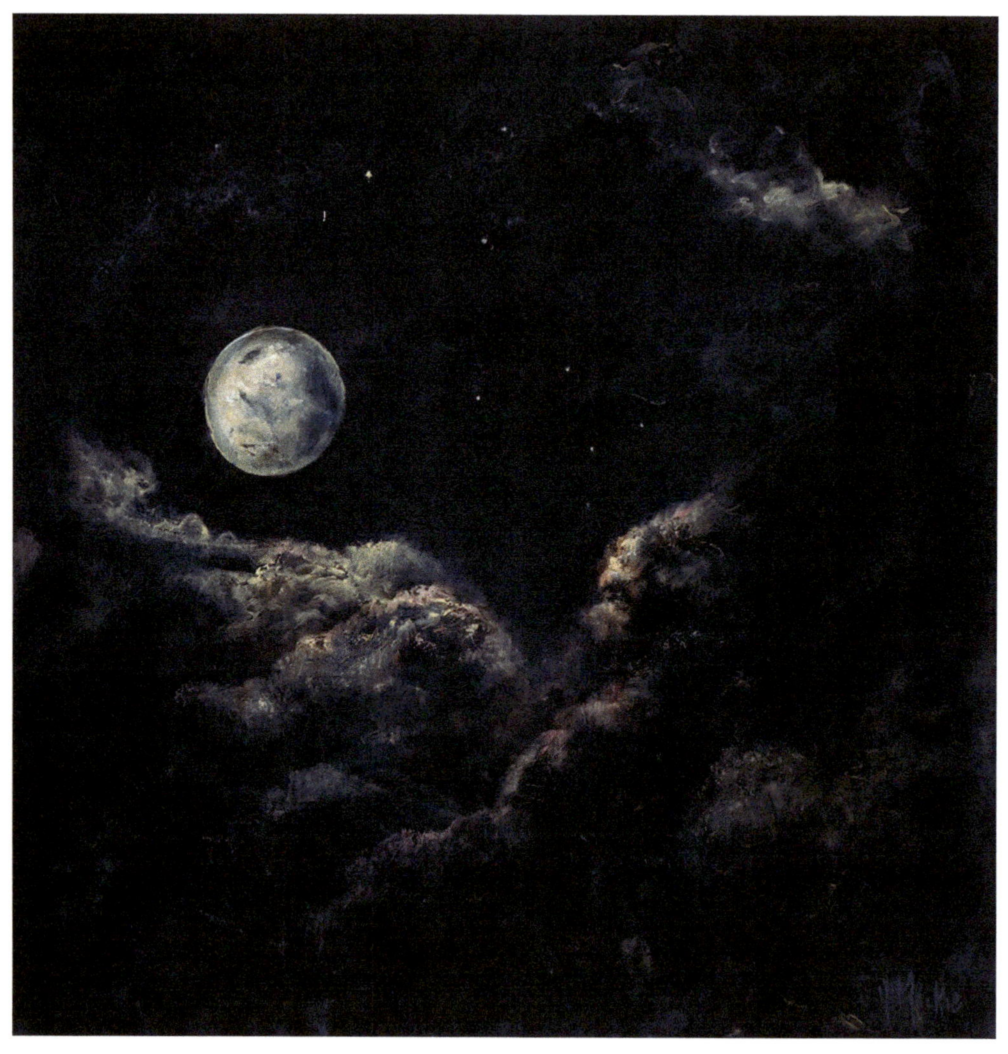

A Starry Night

Moonlight on crests of cloud and beyond, a sky sparkling with stars.

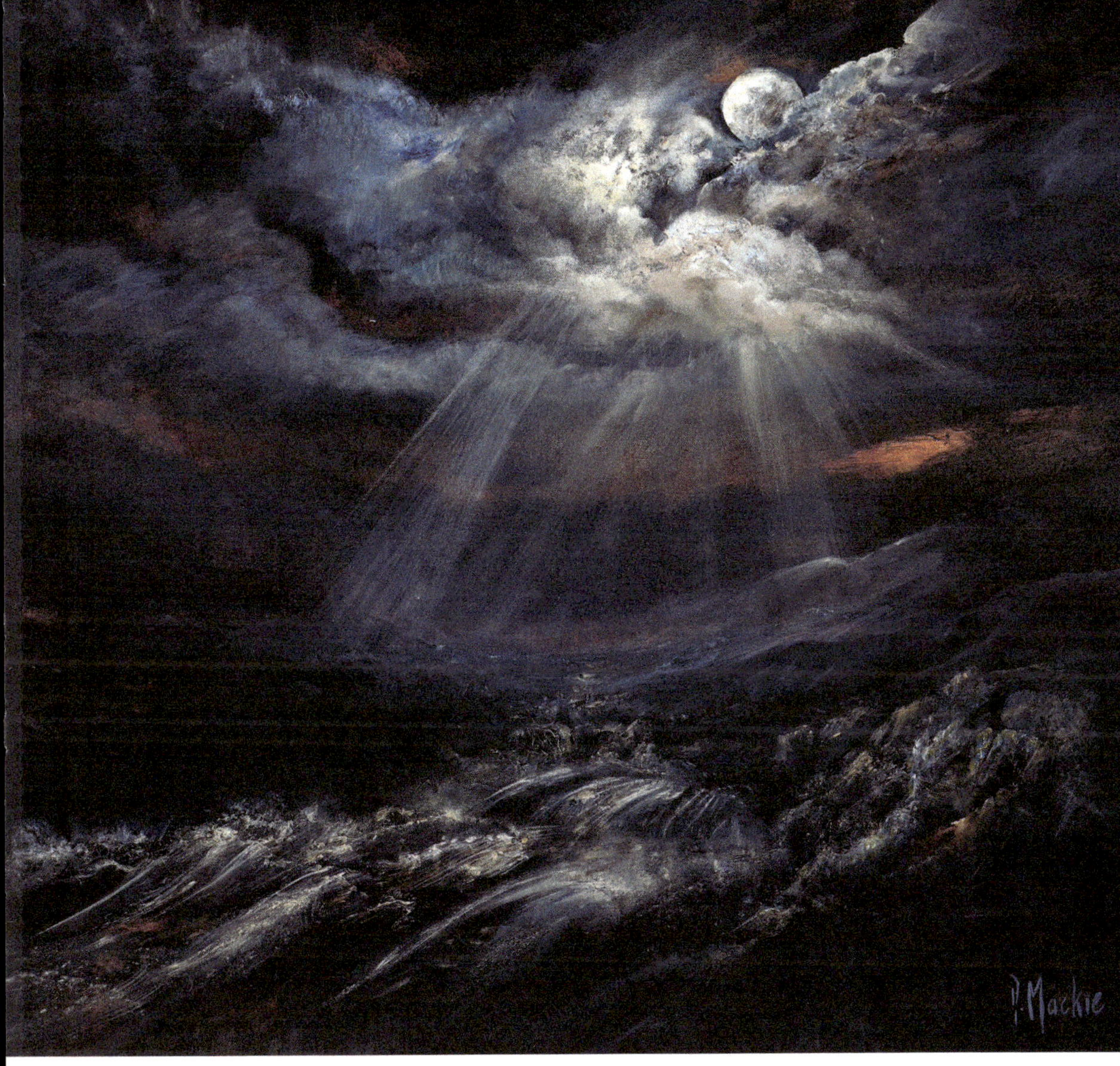

Moonlight Through the Clouds

Moonlight falls on the distant moor, picking out blues and lavenders;
the passage of the swollen burn emphasised by the moonlit spray.

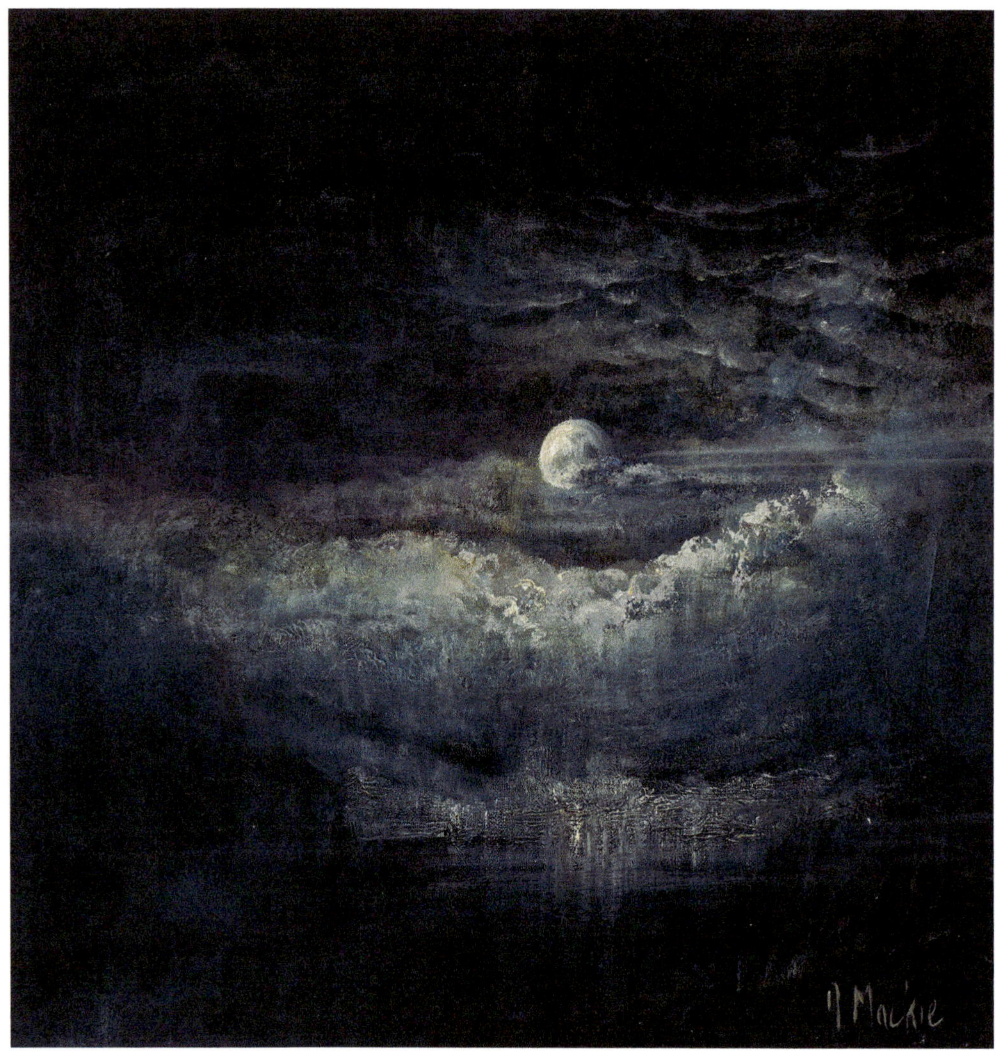

Full Moon

The moon appears to be suspended under a dark quilt and supported by a
luminous one, diffused light falling away into the water beneath.

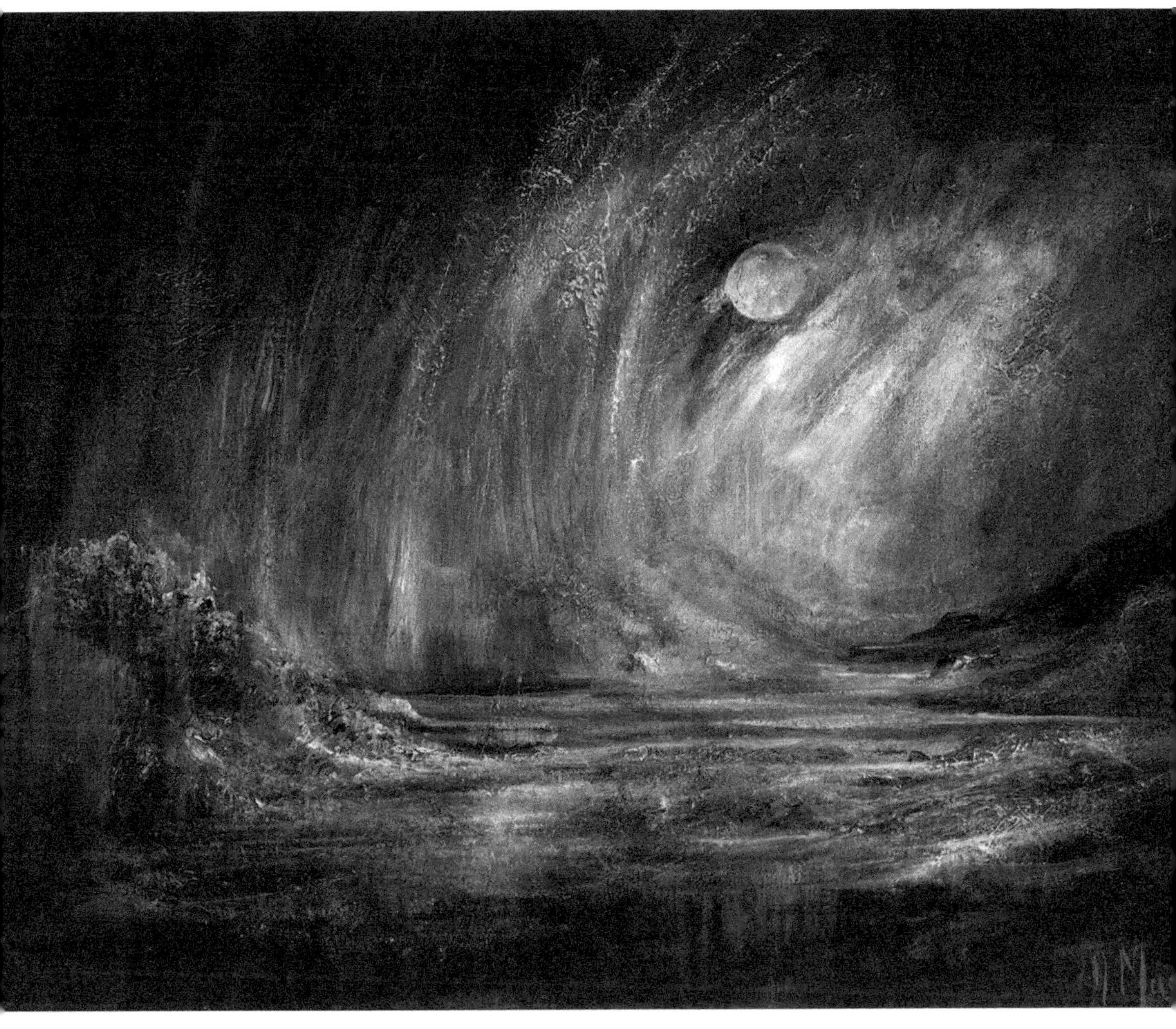

Full Moon and Heavy Rain

The rain lashes down, creating arches of silver that break the surface of the
water and blend into one.

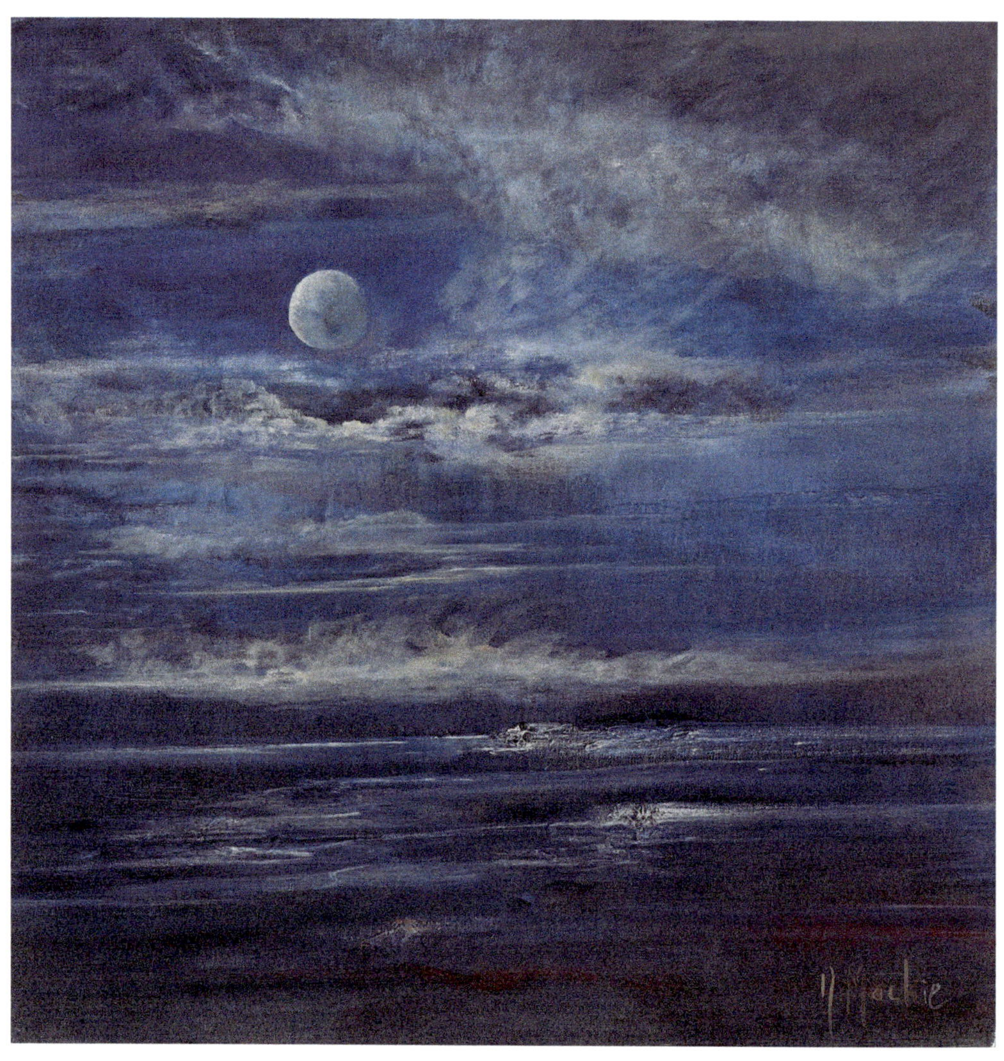

Moonrise, Early Evening

The 'blueness' of the moon's passage across the loch.

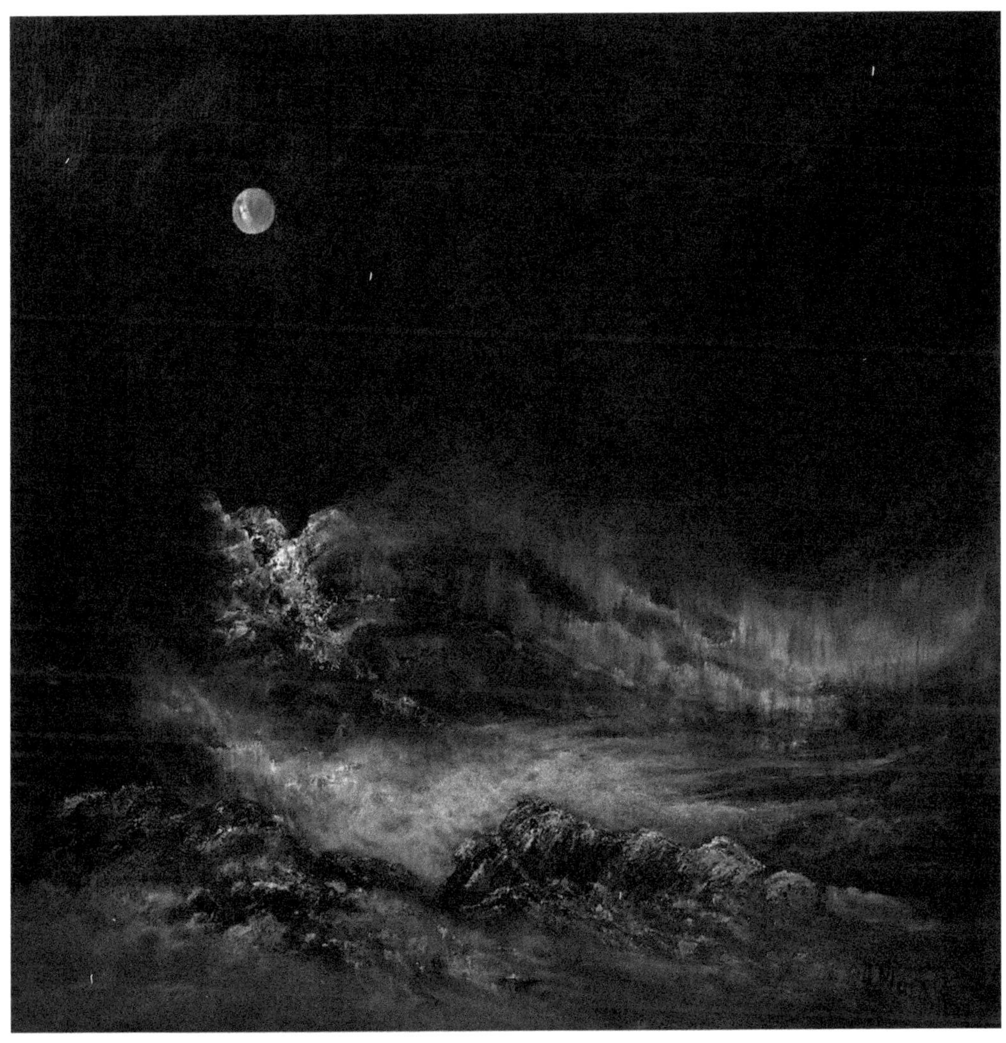

Moonlight and Mists

Mist rolls over the moor under a pale moon.

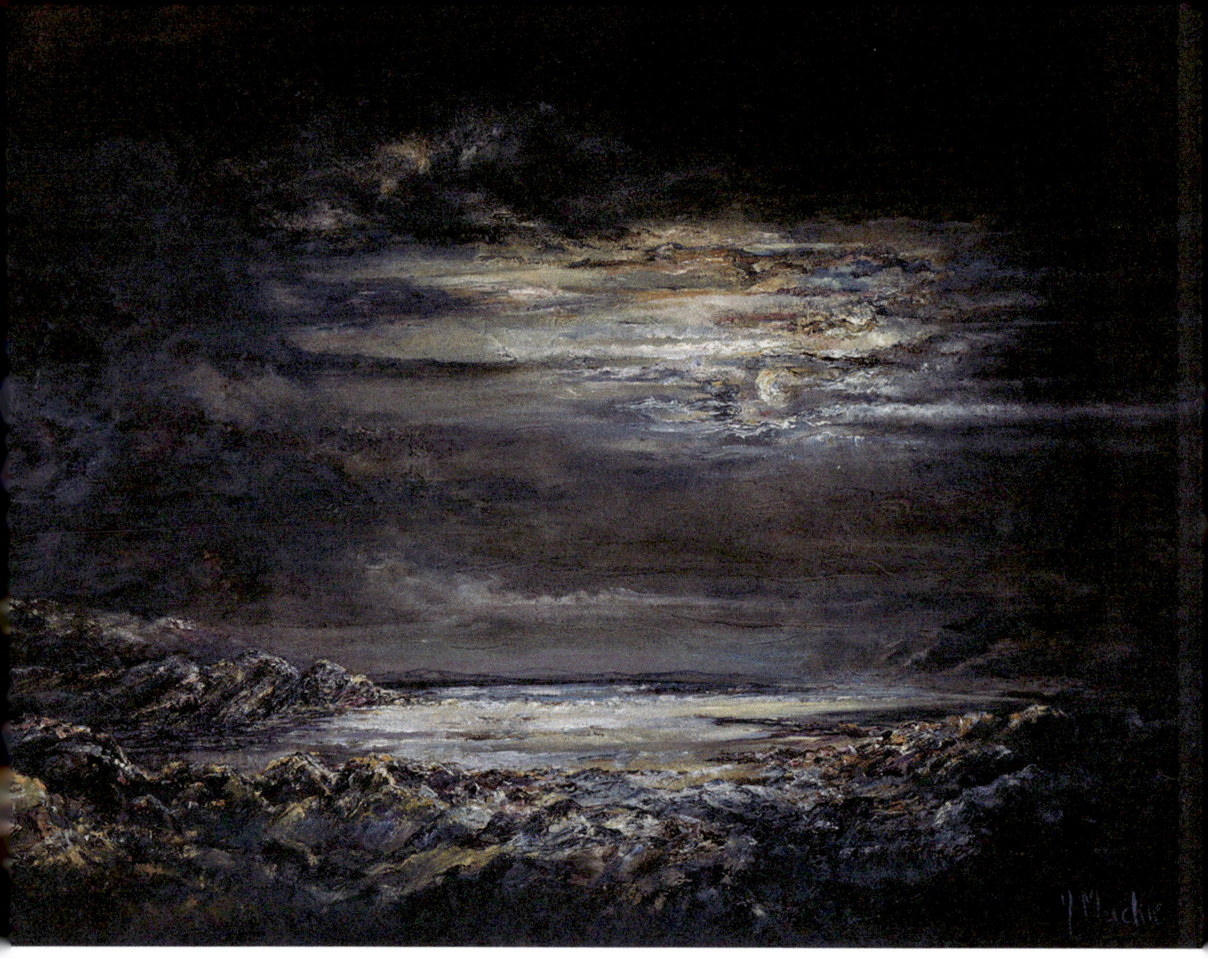

Moonlight on Coral Beach

Vegetative white coral reacts dramatically with the moonlight.

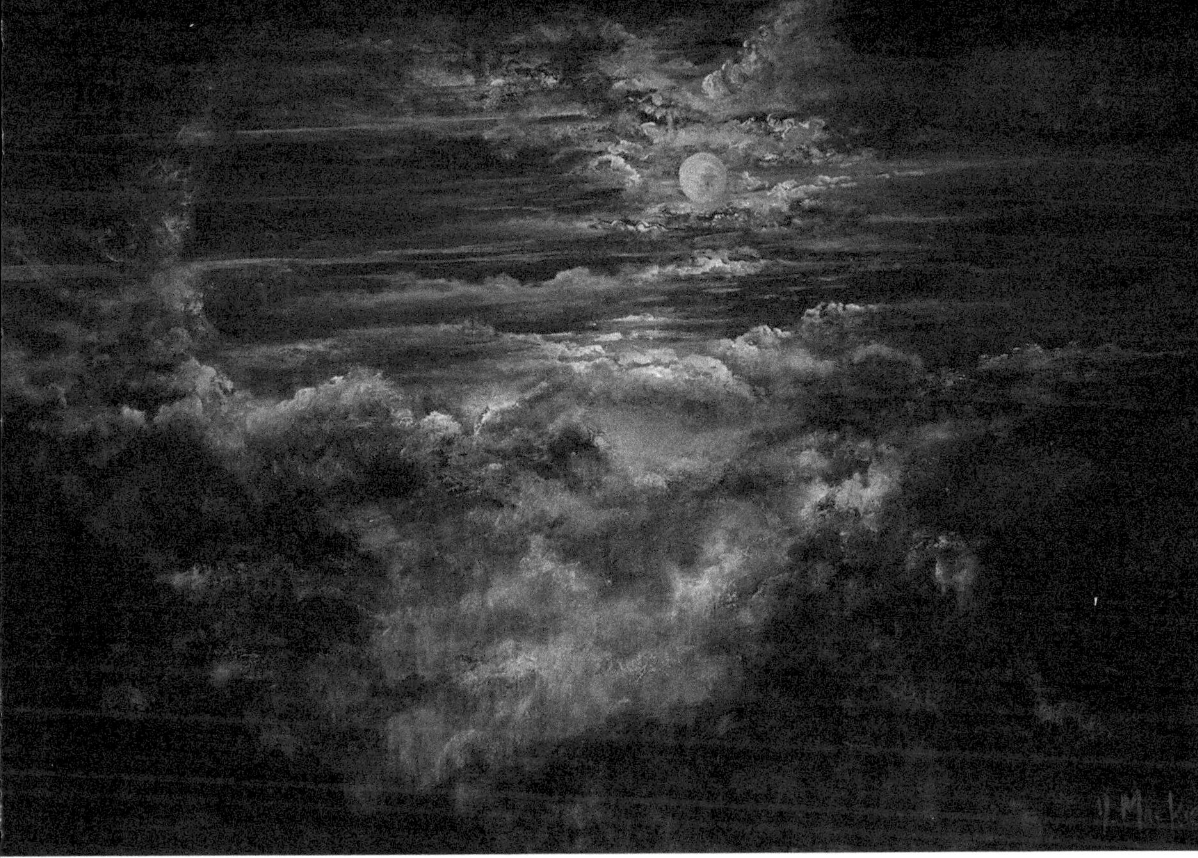

Moonlight and Clouds

Moonlight travelling through a vast depth of cloud, producing subtle tones
both warm and cold.

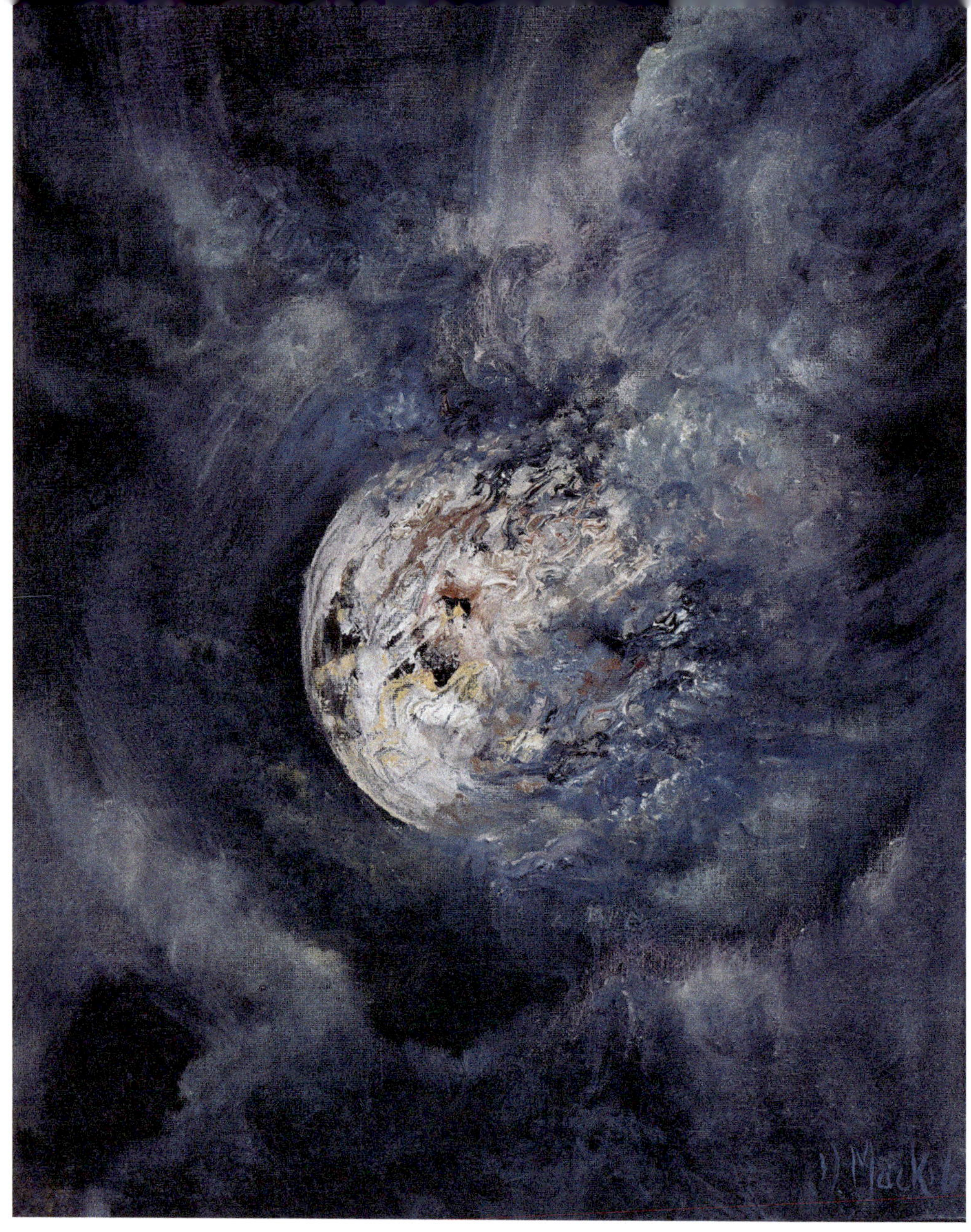

Clouds Clearing (St Petersburg tryptych 1)

The first image of the tryptych gifted to the Arctic Convoy
Museum, St Petersburg. The moon shows her face.

Postscript

The Arctic Convoys: Art for Remembrance

ARTWORKS CAPTURING THE brutal reality of war, such as Picasso's *Guernica* and Goya's *The Disasters of War* prints, can in their graphic intensity be a force for peace in the world. I myself never conceived of creating art for such a purpose until 2018, when I attended a ceremony at Pool House, Poolewe, commemorating the Arctic Convoys, and met some of the veterans. From 1942 until the end of ww2, convoys set out from Loch Ewe on what Churchill called 'the worst journey in the world'; they carried supplies of all sorts, including 4,000 tanks and 7,000 aircraft to support the Russian war effort.

I was utterly inspired and felt a keen desire to do something in honour of their courage. But what could I do that would be of any use at all? For the last two years my paintings had been entirely related to the moon, our silent witness since time began and a symbol of a commonality that surpasses boundaries. The outcome is that Andrey Pritsepov, until recently Russian Consul General in Edinburgh, warmly accepted my offer to donate three paintings to a new museum of the Arctic Convoys in St Petersburg. In one of his emails he noted, 'The moon was considered by the men at sea as a guardian and a sign from heaven.' He was very much in tune with the ultimately hopeful symbolism of these works.

Previously I had known little of this chapter of ww2 history. I was not alone – the story was eclipsed during the Cold War and only recently is the courage of this international force being properly commemorated. In 2018, the Scottish Land Fund awarded £72,820 to the Russian Arctic Convoy Project for premises at Aultbea to house their museum (see russianarcticconvoymuseum.org).

The Russian Arctic Convoys began following a desperate plea from Stalin. Churchill and Roosevelt saw it as vital to the Allies' interests that Russia stay in the war and it is recognised that getting these supplies through turned the tide of battle. American shipyards

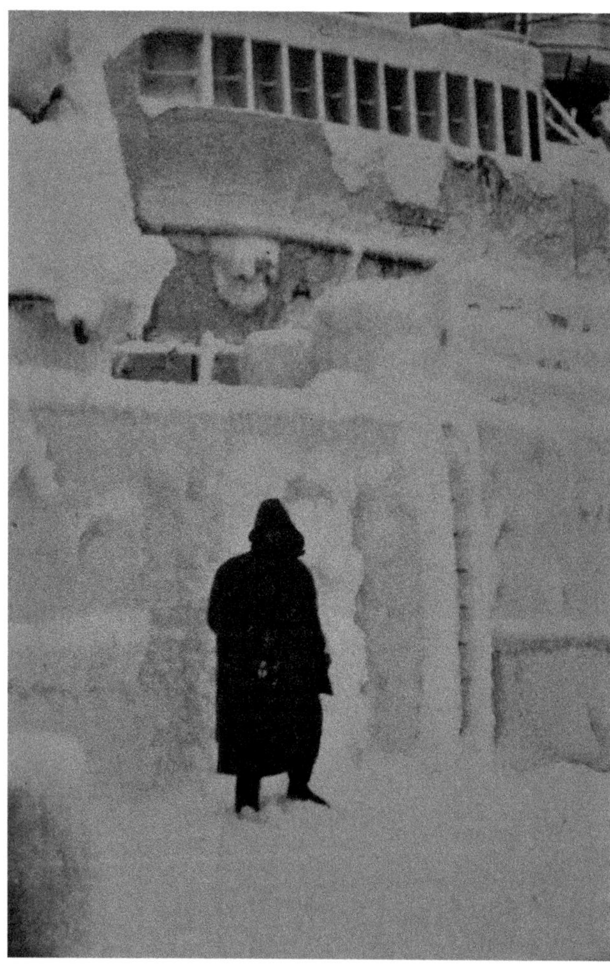

Russian Arctic Convoy Ship

Ice formation made the cargo ships top heavy.

Reproduced courtesy of the Russian Arctic Convoy Museum

built 2,710 Liberty cargo ships between 1941 and 1945. Convoys of about 40 gathered in Loch Ewe before leaving for Russia. I find it fascinating to imagine the residents of the eastern seaboard of Skye witnessing all this as the Liberty ships made their way through the Minch. With military escort, they set out on their perilous journey to Russia, keeping as far as possible from Nazi-occupied Norway and trying to hug the ice further north. This was a double-edged sword: if weather was fine, they could be spotted by reconnaissance aircraft flying out from northern Norway; bad weather, however hazardous, was a kind of safeguard, in that turbulence could throw torpedoes fired from U-boats off course. Typically, conditions were extreme, the crews constantly having to chop ice off decks and rigging. The Germans tried everything to stop the convoys, realising that halting the supply chain could take Russia out of the war. Over 3,000 men were lost on the convoys. In the Russian navy, women also served. On one occasion, a group of female crew members on a tanker that had been torpedoed off Murmansk in north-western Russia defied the order to abandon ship, threatening the captain and first mate with a machine gun to convince them to continue the mission.

The idea to set up a Museum of the Arctic Convoys on the shores of Loch Ewe started with Peter Harrison, the current owner of Pool House. Shortly after he bought it in 1991, he noticed some men gathered nearby and went to speak with them. They turned out to be veterans of the Arctic Convoys and they explained that this place held huge significance for them. The museum now attracts more than 6,000 visitors a year.

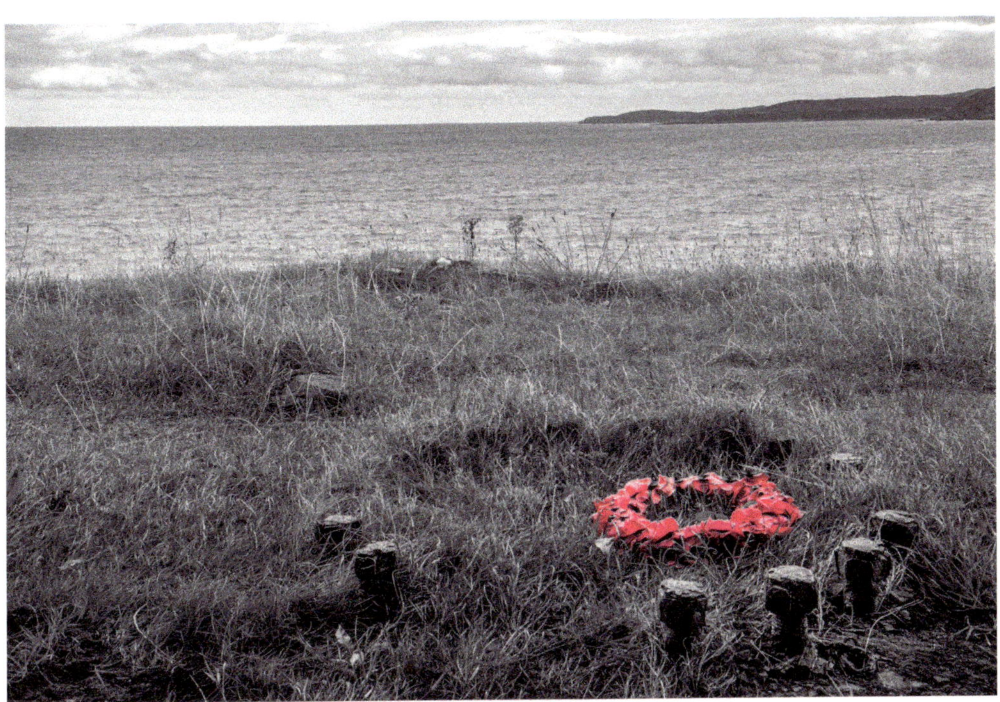

Wreath on the shore of Loch Ewe commemorating the Russian Arctic Convoys

Photo: Adrian Hollister

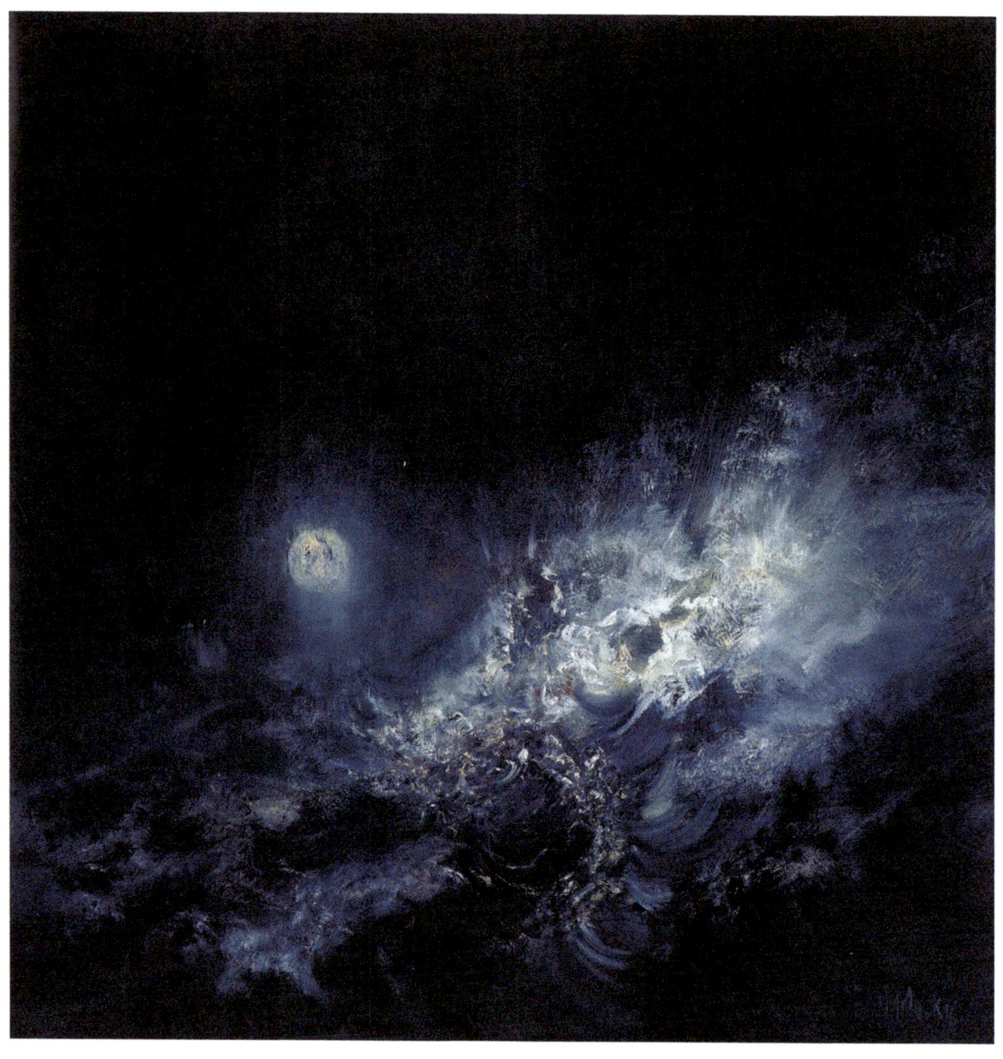

Moon and Surf (St Petersburg tryptych 2)

An image that represents the darkness, terror and acceptance
of death at the hands of our fellow man.

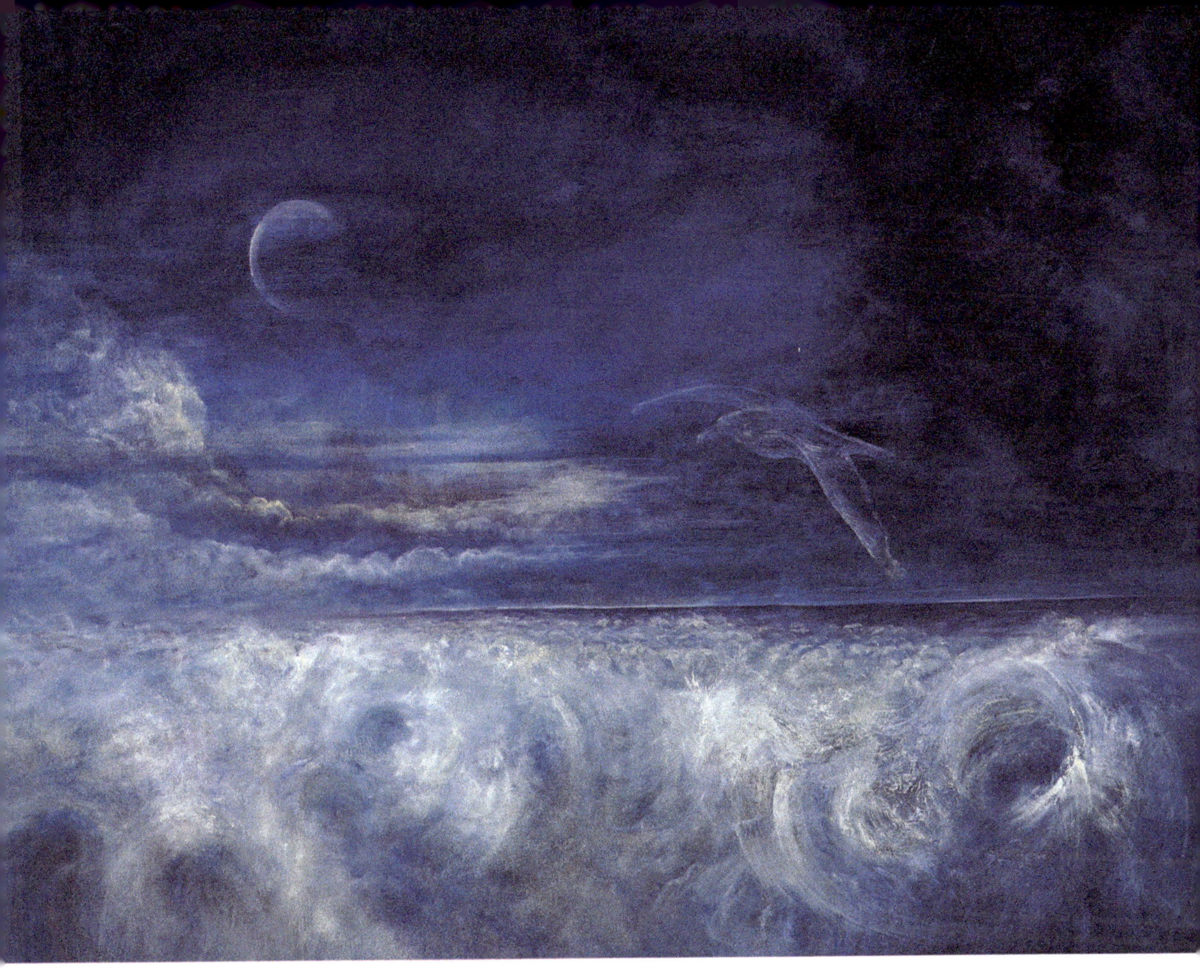

Spirit of the Albatross (St Petersburg tryptych 3)

A new moon just before nightfall. The vibrancy of the light blues
contrasts with the dark and sombre moods of the other two
paintings in the tryptych. The albatross flies towards the light at
that moment of transition between the sun setting and the moon
rising. The bird is ghostly, indicating the presence of past lives
as it flies just above the horizon and a gentle cloud formation
defining calm and peace. In the foreground, tumultuous waves
are breaking under the surface to convey a connection with all
the tragic losses at sea.

Luath Press Limited

committed to publishing well written books worth reading

LUATH PRESS takes its name from Robert Burns, whose little collie Luath (*Gael.*, swift or nimble) tripped up Jean Armour at a wedding and gave him the chance to speak to the woman who was to be his wife and the abiding love of his life. Burns called one of the 'Twa Dogs' Luath after Cuchullin's hunting dog in Ossian's *Fingal*. Luath Press was established in 1981 in the heart of Burns country, and is now based a few steps up the road from Burns' first lodgings on Edinburgh's Royal Mile. Luath offers you distinctive writing with a hint of unexpected pleasures.

Most bookshops in the UK, the US, Canada, Australia, New Zealand and parts of Europe, either carry our books in stock or can order them for you. To order direct from us, please send a £sterling cheque, postal order, international money order or your credit card details (number, address of cardholder and expiry date) to us at the address below. Please add post and packing as follows: UK – £1.00 per delivery address; overseas surface mail – £2.50 per delivery address; overseas airmail – £3.50 for the first book to each delivery address, plus £1.00 for each additional book by airmail to the same address. If your order is a gift, we will happily enclose your card or message at no extra charge.

Luath Press Limited
543/2 Castlehill
The Royal Mile
Edinburgh EH1 2ND
Scotland
Telephone: +44 (0)131 225 4326 (24 hours)
email: sales@luath. co.uk
Website: www. luath.co.uk